The Fourth Branch of Government

BOOKS BY DOUGLASS CATER

Ethics in a Business Society
(*with Marquis W. Childs*)
The Fourth Branch of Government

The Fourth Branch of Government

by Douglass Cater

HOUGHTON MIFFLIN COMPANY BOSTON

The Riverside Press Cambridge

Second printing

Library of Congress Catalog Card Number: 59-7616
Printed in the U.S.A.

To LAC

Preface

⁊ ⁊

INCREASINGLY OF LATE those of us who report from Washington find ourselves the object of curious scrutiny by the political scientists. The press, it has been recognized belatedly, plays an important role in our nation's capital, though nobody seems exactly sure what it is. Too often in past writings the press has been treated, as William Faulkner remarked sardonically, as "that dedicated paladin through whose inflexible rectitude truth shall prevail and justice and mercy be done . . ."

The reporter's role in Washington, which is what my book is about, is a great deal more subtle than this. He is not just the fellow standing on the sidelines, copybook in hand, jotting down the "news" of what is going on. He is heavily involved in the business of government in America.

The gestation of this book has lasted over the nine years I have been a Washington correspondent. Working for *The Reporter,* a fortnightly, I have had an advantageous back seat from which to survey the press as well as politics. The ceaseless interaction of the two is the most continuously unreported story in this heavily reported city.

Two notable assists made the book possible. The first, a fellowship from the John Simon Guggenheim Memorial Foundation, permitted me to conduct the necessary interviews and other research. The second was the award in 1957 of an Eisenhower Fellowship which allowed my wife and me ten months of travel-study in Europe and Asia. Like many others I found that from abroad the image of America grew more clear and that by comparisons and contrasts I began to understand what is distinctive about our system of government.

There are a number who have aided in this book's prolonged birthing: my wife, who has been my valuable research assistant; Max Ascoli, for this, as for my articles in *The Reporter,* the most perceptive of editors; Sidney Hyman, a patient friend and adviser all along the way; the numerous colleagues in the press who have been the willing guinea pigs of this study, and the many others who may not have been so willing. I would like to add a special word of appreciation to Walter Lippmann, whose *Public Opinion* first stimulated my thoughts on this subject, for reading and commenting on the book in manuscript.

D.C.

Contents

The Fourth Branch of Government

I

Government by Publicity

The Nineteenth Century was the era of the novelist. The Twentieth is the era of the journalist. A distracted people, busy with the fierce competitions of modern life, must be addressed while they are paying attention, which is usually at the moment of some great national or international event.

JAMES RESTON*

MORE THAN in any other capital in the world, or any other city in the United States, there is prestige and privilege belonging to the lowly reporter in Washington. Even those who have graduated to the higher callings of columnist or bureau chief still take a modest pride in identifying themselves by the lesser title. Within the press corps, faint derision attaches to one who prefers anything more pretentious.

One aspect of this self-imposed humility — Washington reporters lay great emphasis on the purely physical requirements of the craft. The good reporter, it is said, can be judged by the condition of his legs. Success in the field comes from a fortuitous combination of luck and shoe leather. The business of getting the news is described in the metaphors of the mine worker — pick and shovel, digging, a great deal of sweat. When Hugh Gaitskell, leader of the Labour Party in the British House of Commons, once complained to the erudite

* Quoted by Joe Kraft in "Washington's Most Powerful Reporter," *Esquire,* November 1958.

American columnist Joseph Alsop about the sad condition of parliamentary reporting, Alsop replied: "My dear fellow, the reason is quite simple. Your reporters just don't work as hard as we do!" Alsop, like most columnists, would be mortally insulted to be considered more pundit than reporter.

The Washington correspondent has odd notions about himself. He clings to the image of the reporter as the supreme individual in the age of the organization man. He is the one standing up against the many. He denies stubbornly that the production of news can be likened to the mass production techniques of other large-scale industries. His prestige symbols encourage him in this notion. The Pulitzer Prizes, the Heywood Broun and Raymond Clapper Awards handed out each year go to the reporter who has beaten the system and gotten the "scoop" — to the one who has singlehandedly busted up the hidden enclave of intrigue and purified big government by the cleansing power of publicity.

The myth of the swashbuckling, free-wheeling, heavy drinking general reporter who pursues news with a hunch and a hangover dies hard. It is nourished in the literature of the profession and in the tall tales swapped around the National Press Club bar. But a look at the Press Club — principal gathering place for Washington reporters during off hours — soon dispels the myth. Except for the newspaper mats plastered along the entrance hall, it might be almost any big city eating club, its members as staid and undistinctive. Its consumption at the bar is certainly no heavier than most. If the conversation is a bit more lively, it is because the stock in trade of these merchants is words. Their trade routes often take them to where excitement lies.

The Washington correspondent is a member of a giant industry in the nation's capital, numbering upwards of twelve hundred. His business, like most big business, has become specialized, compartmentalized, channelized, even routinized to a degree that would shock his predecessor of a few decades ago. The growth of the news business has not been simply a stretching out to encompass the broader sphere of government. It has been, in addition, an extension in time and space. News production for the hungry American public has become an instantaneous, continuous, many-faceted and layered operation.

Backbone of the industry and, to a certain extent, its central nervous system are the giant wire services with a labor force large enough to monitor every major news outlet in the capital and to maintain a steady outgoing flow of words. The wire-service employee scarcely conforms to old-fashioned notions of the reporter as one who each twenty-four hours dictates a first draft of history. He is rather the bucket boy for a never ceasing stream of news that may be scooped up at any hour of day or night and poured into print by the far-flung distributors. For him, the news is like fluid, to be portioned out in bulletins, and leads, and "takes." It is capable of being bottled in any quantity. Its production is more determined by the technical than by internal factors in the news itself. The great Associated Press "A" wire that binds the nation can carry an optimum sixty words a minute. News from Washington or London or Hong Kong moves onto it according to tightly scheduled "budgets," scarcely less methodically prepared than a big department store's allotment of display space to shoes and hats and women's lingerie.

Another sizable contingent of the Washington press corps is composed of the "localizers" of the news. They bear daily testament to the fact that the United States has become a world power whose interests are still heavily provincial. These reporters view Washington through the eyes of Dubuque, Iowa, or Kalamazoo, Michigan, or Nashville, Tennessee. They work as one-man vigilantes or as members of large bureaus specializing in perspectives from Maine to Texas. The good ones provide separate eyes and ears for their constituencies — a double check on the Congressmen. Unlike the Congressmen, they can carry even a picayune issue directly to the President with some hope of evoking a response.

There are the Washington bureaus of the big city dailies and the chain papers — highly varied operations ranging from the twenty-three-man princely state maintained by the *New York Times* to the one- and two-man outposts of the Denver *Post* and the Providence *Journal.* These reporters are the most direct spiritual heirs of the long tradition of the Washington correspondent. They, more than the rest, provide the warp and woof of reporting. They range widely in their purpose. For some it is an unending search for scandal and exposé. Some consider their function to be the more leisurely digestion of the raw meat of the headlines.

Other reporters view the Washington scene from other perspectives. Reporters for the news weeklies — artisans on a different type of assembly line from the wire services — dig out the primary components necessary to give a factual shape and color to the week's events. Other components — style, polish, "meaning" — are added further along the assembly line, in the skyscraper workshops of New York. Reporters for radio and television scan the horizon with restless radarscopes in search of news in shapes that can be heard and seen. Syndicated columnists, the most independent of the news merchants, batter the barricades for their "inside" news purveyed on a thrice or more weekly basis and ranging in content from foreign policy to freight rates. The foreign press corps works with varying success to chart America's course for their constituents.

A trade press in considerable numbers sifts the capital city for the particular nuggets that will be of value to the organized interest groups keeping a relentless vigil over the government. This is not to mention the large group who pursue their living in the demi-world between journalism and out-and-out lobbying.

Within the larger Washington news bureau, government is a complex organization chart broken into sectors familiarly known as "beats." A recent assignment sheet of the Associated Press, for example, indicates the degree of compartmentalization:

> Senate, 6 reporters; House of Representatives, 5; Supreme Court, 1; Pentagon and Atomic Energy Commission, 2; State Department, 3; White House, 1 or 2; Aviation, 1; Treasury, Federal Reserve and Commerce, 1; business news, 1; Justice and Transportation Commissions (ICC and FCC), 1; Labor, NLRB, and labor unions, 1; Interior, Welfare and outlying Agencies, 1; regional staff, 20; world news, 7; and special features, 7.

Each beat has its prescribed routines. Within the government agencies, frequently within an agency's divisions and subdivisions, there are information offices to provide a point of contact for the reporter. The number of government information officers, who stand ready to "brief" him, totals close to three thousand, it has been estimated, or more than twice the number of the press corps itself. The reporter on the beat must devote a sizable amount of time to culling the massive documentary of "handouts" — i.e., mimeographed press releases — which represents the government's own idea of what the news should be.

But his work is by no means limited to this channelized intercourse with government. In Washington the reporter who limits his enterprise to use of the press agent and the handout is considered a slacker. He is expected to break through to other sources of information. He must "go upstairs" and query the policy makers in person. The reporter is outraged if he experiences difficulty in seeing Cabinet members or other political appointees. Even the career civil servant at the upper levels learns to be accessible to the press. Though it is not listed in his job specification, his career may well depend on his ability to feed information to reporters during critical policy struggles.

Reporting has grown complex and technical along with everything else. Take, for example, the shadings of attribution that can be given the source of a reporter's story — "high government officials," "informed circles," or simply "It was learned that . . ." The "leak" has become institutionalized. There is the background briefing, deep background, and off-the-record. Reporting has become ritualized. The open press conference has turned into a mass convocation, its usefulness often impeded by the hordes of reporters who feel duty-bent on being present to write down, to tape and to film all that occurs.

Reporting of government, like all big businesses, has its good points and its bad ones so far as the employee is concerned. The work habits are not so fixed as most, less adaptable to the time clock, more susceptible to peak and slack periods. The pay scale starts higher but advances more slowly than in comparable occupations. Those at the top — bureau chiefs, columnists, and certain well-known special correspondents — are paid very well, though not nearly so well as the elite in such roughly comparable activities as advertising and public relations. For the rank and file, the wage scale is by no means a major incentive.

The reporter in Washington finds in journalism a career that becomes no less physically demanding and little more remunerative as he reaches middle age. Each year's spill-over of weary correspondents into some form of public relations activities is high.

Other incentives hold the Washington correspondent to

his trade. To judge by his own admission, they can be quite trivial. He finds the same thrill in chasing after the news event as the firehorse gets at the sound of the gong. There is ego satisfaction in seeing one's name at the head of a column of print. The reporter has an opportunity to associate on a fairly intimate basis with high officials and politicians.

But these, I submit, do not constitute the basic incentives of a substantial group of correspondents in Washington who show extraordinary devotion to the task of reporting government. They have done little to articulate for themselves or for others what is their motivation. It can only be discovered in their casual conversation.

They have an acute sense of involvement in the churning process that is government in America. The reporter is the recorder of government but he is also a participant. He operates in a system in which power is divided. He as much as anyone, and more than a great many, helps to shape the course of government. He is the indispensable broker and middleman among the subgovernments of Washington. He can choose from among the myriad events that seethe beneath the surface of government which to describe, which to ignore. He can illumine policy and notably assist in giving it sharpness and clarity; just as easily, he can prematurely expose policy and, as with an undeveloped film, cause its destruction. At his worst, operating with arbitrary and faulty standards, he can be an agent of disorder and confusion. At his best, he can exert a creative influence on Washington politics.

In no other major capital does the reporter have quite this political role. Patrick O'Donovan, correspondent for the London *Observer,* has commented:

> Most strangers are astonished by the power of the American and, more particularly, the Washington press. It fulfills an almost constitutional function. And it works with a seriousness and responsibility which — even though it may lack the

> luxuries of style — cannot be matched in Britain today . . . The process has been many years in developing. It has produced a small group of writers who must be included in any outline of what constitutes "Washington" . . . They not only check and when necessary destroy individuals, they positively affect the course of policy. The inner group of them is privileged — a few by the Administration, most by the opposition that always exists even within the Civil Service and the Forces. They tend to be scholarly and are judged solely by their accuracy and the richness of their ideas. Without them, the idea of Washington could well be a dangerous one.

⁂

During the latter years of the Truman Administration the widely publicized challenge to presidential leadership arising in Congress aroused deep concern among those anxious about America's role in the free-world alliance. Yet, viewed with the hindsight of a very few years, it was a challenge that contained a curious contradiction. The President, even at the lowest ebb of his political fortunes, maintained a program and a budget that would have appeared grandiose to most earlier Presidents. The office of the President held a degree of paramountcy over legislative planning that never even existed before the time of Franklin D. Roosevelt. It is doubtful whether a single prerogative of the Presidency was actually diminished.

What had in fact happened was that the focus of public attention shifted from the White House to the committee rooms of Congress. Prior to 1950, the major events of government attracting the public attention included the Truman Doctrine, the Marshall Plan, Point Four, the Berlin Airlift, and the North Atlantic Treaty Organization with its accompanying Military Defense Assistance Program — all executive-inspired and carried out with the "advice and consent" of Congress. Then, in June 1950, there was the President's decision to send American troops to Korea.

But even before this display of presidential initiative, there had commenced on Capitol Hill a series of spectacles the effect of which was to make Congress, not the President, the principal source of news and explanation and opinion. In any newsman's book the major Washington stories from 1950 to 1953 would include the Tydings investigation of the McCarthy charges, the MacArthur dismissal inquiry, the McCarran hearings, and Senator McCarthy's continuing warfare against the State Department. Even the news of a new President was almost obscured by the continued uproar from Capitol Hill. In all of this, of course, the Executive Branch of government played an active, if reluctant, role. But the staging, the judging, and the issuing of most pronouncements came from Congress or, more specifically, from certain members and groups in Congress.

It is important, I believe, to examine the consequences of this shift in public attention. The investigations themselves were singularly barren of conclusions. Despite all the furor, they did not result in drastic legislative reforms or even in substantial defeats to the Administration's foreign program. Yet, it would be idle to claim that this shift had not affected the balance of power in American government. It served to diminish the usefulness of a great many of the President's chief lieutenants and to elevate into positions of commanding importance hitherto obscure members of Congress. It enabled one comparatively junior Senator lacking the conventional trappings of seniority and prestige to sustain for a considerable time a threat to the President's control over the Executive Branch. It created serious doubts at home and abroad whether the President did in fact stand at the helm of government during a critical time in world affairs.

This era, in brief, illustrates that the way government is publicized can be of major importance. We have today what might be called government by publicity. It has grown with the growth of modern mass communications and public opinion polling — twin technologies that seek to revive the Aristotelian concept of the citizen as firsthand spectator and participant in the marketplace of government. Publicity is a force uniquely indispensable to the American system in which "public opinion" is called on daily to arbitrate between the two competing branches of government supposedly separate and coordinate according to what Woodrow Wilson called the "literary theory" of our Constitution.

In recent years the United States government has, in fact, experienced a curious turnabout in the exercise of powers from what was envisaged in constitutional doctrine. The President, aided by a growing staff of experts, has become the prime formulator of legislative program. Congress, on the other hand, with the proliferation of its investigative committees ever attempts to serve as board of review and veto over the ordinary administration of the Executive departments. Each, in testing the undefined limits of these new-claimed prerogatives, must resort unceasingly to public explanation to sustain the logic of its claims.

Within the Executive Branch itself, grown large and infinitely fragmented, the publicity competition frequently takes on the character of a life and death struggle. Inside the Pentagon, where a sizable chunk of the federal budget is divided up, the highest classifications of military secrecy often go out the window in the rivalry among the three services. When an Army Colonel was recently court-martialed for leaking to the press secret information about the Army missile Jupiter, Dr. Wernher von Braun, head of the Army Missile Program, testified in his defense, "The Jupiter involves several million dollars of the taxpayers' money. One hundred per cent security would mean no information for the public, no money for the Army, no Jupiter . . . The Army has got to play the same game as the Air Force and the Navy." [1]

The competitive drive of men to attract public attention in order to attain political power is, of course, as old as politics itself. What is comparatively recent and, I believe, peculiar to the American system is the way in which publicity affects not only men and policies but the fundamental balances of government itself.

This analysis would have little point if the publicity system could be assumed to convey a precise image of government — if the shadows cast on the cave's wall for the citizen to see retained a rigid proportion to the reality they reflect. But this is by no means the case. As anyone who spends time in Washington surely comes to learn, the business of publicity is no more automatic nor free from artifice than the business of government itself. Indeed, there are built-in biases that all too frequently make the images of government transmitted to the public take on strange and unnatural shapes. On occasion, publicity has been known to assume a generative spirit of its own — in turn re-creating the people and policies being publicized even as the Hollywood starlet is remade to fit the public stereotype.

The reporter in Washington has witnessed on numerous occasions the phenomenon described by the psychologist when the mask of the man takes possession of the true self. More than witness, he has helped to shape the mask which transforms the public figure. Many observed the phenomenal "growth" of Senator John McClellan, an obscure and occasionally demagogic politician until the time of the McCarthy extravaganzas. Undoubtedly McClellan in a time of challenge discovered hitherto unrealized sources of strength within himself. But close observers also noted a tendency in

[1] *New York Times,* June 27, 1957.

the Senator to live up to the heroic proportions attributed to him by certain prominent columnists.

A leading correspondent, who prefers to remain anonymous, has provided a revealing testament to this creative function in a letter to a friend:

> I have had one very important experience in this town. I knew Arthur Vandenberg when I thought he was the most pompous and prejudiced man in the United States Senate. I saw him change partly by the processes of mellowing old age, but mainly by accident and particularly as a result of public reaction to his famous speech of January 10, 1945. I happen to know that that speech, or rather the main parts of it, were largely accidental. I can say to you privately that I was, myself, quite by chance responsible for that change in the speech. But my point is that what changed Vandenberg was not the speech itself, but the press of public reaction to the speech, and from then on, as you know, he played an important and perhaps a decisive role in winning bipartisan support for the concept of collective security.

What the writer failed to add was that the "press of public reaction" was in large part stimulated by the tremendous fanfare given by leading newspapers to Vandenberg's speech, a build-up that took the Senator quite by surprise, as he confessed in his private papers, published posthumously. It was not the first time — or the last — that the Washington journalist has hailed the policy declaration which he himself had a hand in ghosting.

This creative power of publicity cannot be explained solely by the fact that in a democracy publicity influences public opinion, which in turn must ever be a determining influence on government. There are ways of short-cutting the classic workings of democracy. In an age of complex and fast-breaking events, the measurement of publicity comes to be taken as a cheap and convenient substitute for public opinion. For the politician and the bureaucrat the headline inch frequently serves as the day-to-day measure of public opinion on a great number of issues. By their responses to this synthetic public opinion they stimulate further publicity and so commences a reflexive cycle that has been known to move news stories from the inside to the front page and to reshape policies as surely as if public opinion had exerted its sovereign will.

To study the publicity process in government means to study the ways and means by which government explains itself to the people. It also means necessarily to study the news-forming habits and techniques of the press, radio, and television, which transmit most of the public explanation of government. It means to examine the definition of news itself. Just as individual man cannot communicate thoughts that lie beyond the limits of his vocabulary to express, so it might be said that the vocabulary of the press delimits the thinking of men in organized society, particularly on matters as remote to their daily experience as their national government.

It is strange that the political scientist has so long neglected the study of the interaction between government and the press. The American Fourth Estate operates as a *de facto,* quasiofficial fourth branch of government, its institutions no less important because they have been developed informally and, indeed, haphazardly. Twelve hundred or so members of the Washington press corps, bearing no authority other than accreditation by a newspaper, wire service, or network, are part of the privileged officialdom in the nation's capital. The senior among them claim a prestige commensurate with their continuing power. For Presidents come and go but press bureau chiefs are apt to remain a while.

The power they exercise is continuing and substantive. They are the articulators of those events of government which they and their bosses deem worthy of note. Their strength stems from their ability to select — to define what is news and what isn't. In Washington on an average day, a good many hundreds of thousands of words are spoken, tens of dozens of "events" occur. The press decides which of those words and events shall receive the prompt attention of millions and which, like timber falling in a deep and uninhabited forest, shall crash silently to the ground.

The reporter in Washington has prerogatives belonging to journalists in no other capital. He has access to the Chief Executive. At the White House press conference, he determines by his questions which matters shall be brought to the President's attention and in what way. The reporters, not the President, ultimately decide which of the President's utterances are headlined to the nation, which given lesser treatment, and which pretty well ignored.

The President, of course, gives the ritual of the press conference its basic content. But the reporters largely determine the form. It is a source of continual amazement to the uninitiated how loosely defined are the ground rules for interrogating our head of state.

The reporter serves as one systematic channel of communication between Congress and the Executive which continues to function when others have broken off. Through him the opposition as well as lesser members of the President's own party can bring their queries to the President's ear with some certainty of a response. Conversely, select reporters enjoy an intimacy with the congressional leaders that few members of the White House staff ever share.

In times of critical congressional debate, when the hour for voting draws near, the rooms outside the chambers become a beehive of whispered consultation between press and politician. News tickers in the Capitol and White House lobbies transmit the last-minute communiqués. The hastily torn off teletape rushed to the Senate floor is a familiar sight during the final frenzied assaults on the enemies' strongholds. As each congressional fight reaches its crisis, one is made sharply aware of the pervasive influence of news and newsmen.

No one who has been in on the development and growth of a major policy is likely to minimize the publicity consciousness which must guide its course every step of the way. At a gathering of newsmen to pay honor to him for his famous Plan, General George C. Marshall gave an unsolicited testimonial to this. "I found as in everything I touched almost, particularly in military operations, it is not so hard to make a general plan; the great problem is how to put that thing over; how you carry it through, and that was the case in this instance." Marshall went on to spell out those problems of putting across the Marshall Plan which have lingered in his memory. He told of his concern at the time of his speech at Harvard in June 1947, lest the conservative Middle West rise up to veto the Plan before it had got off the ground. What he had not anticipated and what proved to be a tremendous boon to the Plan was the immediate response of the European leaders to his speech. "The result of Messieurs Bevin and Bidault's anticipation of the Plan provoked so much reaction that the Middle West was forgotten for a month and a half," Marshall declared.

Of course, the Middle West was not forgotten at all, least of all by the people in the Middle West. But what really happened was that the great floodlights of the press were concentrated on the European news events rather than searching out, and perhaps stimulating, news events from Ohio.

This tendency for the development of news to influence reactively the development of the events on which it feeds should not be minimized. It is a force that cannot be precisely charted. It can be a result of pure chance. It can, as modern practitioners of the art of public relations appreciate, be made the object of manipulation. It can even be a product of conscious cooperation from the press. At the gathering in Marshall's honor, Paul Hoffman paid glowing tribute to certain members of the Washington press corps. "We would have never gotten the dollars," said Hoffman, "if it hadn't been for the support of the reporters of the Overseas Writers Club." The tribute was duly accepted by the members present, including representatives of the passionately objective wire services. There are many moments in a reporter's workday when he silently accepts the fact that the formulation of news is not exactly a scientific process foreign to the reporter's thoughts and feelings and ambitions.

The reporter works within limits. News is a vaguely definable commodity recognized more by instinct perhaps than by copybook maxims. One of the perennial sources of astonishment for the nonprofessional is to attend a congressional committee hearing and witness the row upon row of reporters seated at the press tables as they lift their pencils and lay them down with almost ballet corps precision while the flow of testimony moves along. The skilled reporter's measurement of "news" is not simply defined by what goes into the total story. It can be charted by which chunk goes into the "lead," which is buried in the tail, and which, with squirrel-like foresight, is tucked away for the "overnight." The dogmas of what is "news" help determine the priorities of what is communicated to the public about its government.

News standards go to the very core of policy formulation by officials. As a program moves from the tentative planning stage in the Executive department through the long wearisome process of legislative enactment, appropriation, further enactment, and still further appropriation, there is an inevitable tendency to accentuate those aspects which are newsworthy and to de-emphasize — sometimes causing atrophy — those aspects which are not newsworthy.

The competitive news advantage of one policy over another has great bearing on the comparative ease with which each survives the legislative process. Under the vast panoply of our foreign aid programs, military assistance with its newsworthy qualities — its marching troops, long lines of tanks, and low sweeping planes — has a publicity appeal which aids greatly its continuation. On the contrary, a worthy program like economic aid requires tremendous exertion to seek out its newsworthy traits, vast oversimplification, and the mammoth efforts of private groups who zealously exploit the small news potential in order to develop political support. Congressional ardor in approaching these two programs bears a direct relationship.

It is impossible to chart precisely the conforming influence of publicity upon policy. A few who were privy to the initial formulation of the Marshall Plan discovered that publicity requirements as much as anything else dictated its evolution from a program directed against "hunger and want" to one aimed more concretely at Communism. It was perhaps a subtle shift of emphasis but far-reaching in its effect.

It is useful to examine the basic conflict of interest that exists between government and the press. A more detailed inquiry into the nature of this conflict will be left to later chapters. Here I would simply point out that the official and the reporter are moved by fundamentally different compulsions. The official's first response to a newsworthy event is assimilative. He attempts to relate it to the broad body of record on which he precariously builds his policies. The reporter's first impulse, on the other hand, is distributive: he seeks to communicate the newsworthy event as speedily and widely as possible.

Inside the Executive Branch official cables, coded and decoded, lag by vital hours and sometimes days the dispatches of the press. On a weekend in 1955 the Undersecretary of

State, acting in his superior's absence from the city, learns through a press report that Chinese Communist leader Chou En-lai has made a bid for negotiation on the Formosa Straits dispute. He knows, too, that the American public has been similarly informed. The press stands ready to take down, even insistent on receiving his response. The Undersecretary has not received an official report from the field evaluating the proposal, but he does not want to give the "publicity play" to the Communists over the weekend. He drafts a hurried reply summarily knocking down the Communist bid. It turns out that he has not had time to gauge the full import of Chou En-lai's proposal or to conceive a skillful answer. The Secretary, on his return, makes an effort to rectify the blunder. In this case, the priorities of the press have hustled the procedures of government.

The official must think in terms of finding the lowest common denominator of agreement. For him the business of policy making is a matter of accommodation. Particularly as it reaches the topmost levels of government, there is need to fuzz over disagreements in the quest for a sense of unanimity. Regular participants at meetings of the National Security Council, the nation's highest strategic body, testify that the problem frequently reduces itself to finding the phrase of appropriate subtlety to bridge unnecessary conflicts. The official, as Dean Acheson has remarked, remembers the words of Justice Holmes: "Some things have got to be stated obscurely before they can be stated clearly."

For the reporter, the basic quest is to discover and highlight traces of disunity. As a government official once complained, the reporter is Hegelian. He thinks in terms of thesis and antithesis. It is his premise that progress comes through controversy and that truth, as has been said, is generated by encounter as fire is made by rubbing together two sticks.

The official acts on the premise that premature publicity can be a destructive force if it undermines the effort to reconcile diverse interests and causes the hardening of fixed positions. The reporter believes in the purifying powers of publicity. He is the sworn enemy of secrecy. He holds firm in the faith that "public opinion" must have an opportunity to express itself while policy is still malleable and has not been molded into unchangeable dogma.

Arthur Krock, columnist of the *New York Times,* has summed up succinctly the conflicting mandates of newspaperman and official:

> Our obligations are merely these in deciding whether to go into print with information: Is it true? Has it been legitimately acquired? Is it fit to print — public property or a private matter? These satisfactorily settled, the facts are ready for their bath of printer's ink.
>
> But the statesman has other considerations. Is it premature? Will publication make the going more difficult? Will publication tend to confuse, rather than to clarify, the popular mind? These are some of the problems before him, particularly if he is President of the United States in a catastrophic hour, forcing the innermost fibers of his body and the full resources of his spirit into his colossal task.

It is interesting to note that in the Soviet Union there is no such dichotomy between the reporter and the commissar. By Communist definition, the press is an instrument of state and party for the "education" of the people. News can be held in a state of suspension for weeks or months without losing its newsworthiness when the decision to publish is finally made. Despite its lip service to a philosophy of dialectical materialism, the Soviet press has invented a whole new vocabulary to describe its government in nondialectical terms. Socialist progress as reported in *Pravda* is a straight-line proposition.

The Soviet reporter will admit of no conflict of interest between government and the press.

But for American government, this conflict is very real. On Dean Acheson's last day in office as Secretary of State, he was paid a visit by James Reston, Washington correspondent for the *New York Times*. The purpose of Reston's call was to ask quite bluntly why the Secretary and he had not enjoyed better working relations. Underlying his question was the unhappy conviction that Acheson, who brought unusually high talents to the office, had been unwittingly caught in the riptides of publicity. The Secretary's effectiveness had been gradually eroded by failures of communication.

Secretary Acheson answered equally bluntly that what Reston suggested would have been impossible, since there was a basic conflict of purpose between the two of them. A Secretary of State, Acheson said, has to germinate new policies and to nurse them along until they have reached the stage of development when they can withstand the battering assaults of the political arena. The reporter's primary purpose, on the other hand, is to get news for his paper no matter what the effect on policy.

Reston stoutly denies that the conflict can be defined in quite these terms. He admits it is the duty of the reporter to get at the news while it is still news. In government today, when so many policy decisions are made in the closed precincts of the Executive departments, the press would be abdicating its function if it were to sit by until these decisions are formally announced. But Reston argues that Secretary Acheson failed to understand and make use of the creative power of the press to muster public support for sound policy and, alternatively, to gauge the full extent of public reaction to unsound or unrealistic policy.

This dialogue between the Secretary and the reporter — both able and earnest men, both anxious that democratic government should be effective government — reveals a dilemma of government and the press in a free society. It is a dilemma more recognizable in the United States than in the parliamentary democracies where the press does not play so intimate a role in the scheme of things. It afflicts Republican and Democratic administrations alike for it has nothing to do with partisan affiliations of government or the press.

There are other dilemmas. With the growth of big government and of modern mass techniques for communicating the news about government, there has been a parallel growth in the subtle art of manipulating the flow of information. To a remarkable extent, the public trust nowadays is afflicted with an acute public relations sense. The tendency to "manage the news" on the part of those having a particular interest in it disturbs and frequently confounds the best of reporters.

The following chapters describe in more detail our system of government by publicity and the challenge it poses for reporters and responsible public officials alike. I have tried to avoid harsh judgments or hasty panaceas. Certainly, the institutions of both government and the free press in America are equally ancient and inviolable. Much of the tension between the two is part of the healthy unrest of democracy.

Yet both need to be examined to discover how much or how little they contribute to a continuing disorder in democracy which results in weakness rather than strength. It is a failure for democracy when government fails to explain itself clearly and candidly to the citizens. It is equally a failure when the press fails to communicate intelligibly the news of government or when that news becomes a propaganda weapon employed by self-seeking interests to frustrate effective leadership in a democracy.

2

The President and the Press

> He is, or can be, the essence of the nation's personality. In him, many things can flower — or decay.
>
> SIDNEY HYMAN*

NO MONARCH in history has had a retinue like that which gathers about the American President and calls itself the White House press corps. The reporters hang about his antechamber with the indolence of courtiers at some feudal court keeping those who pass in and out — Governors, Cabinet members, Senators, Ambassadors — under constant surveillance and interrogation. They dog the President's every step and turn his most casual public conversation into a mass meeting. They follow him wherever he goes. Their special plane takes off after the one carrying him and alights just in advance of it. Thus even the contingency of a fatal crack-up has been calculated so as not to interrupt the flow of prompt and plentiful publicity about our President.

No television idol, axe-murderer, or foreign head of state lives in the glare of continual publicity that is the accepted fate of our President. His ordinary habits of work and play are the grist of ever fresh "news" from the White House. His most minor indispositions turn the place into a mecca for

* In *The American President* (New York, 1954).

journalistic pilgrims prepared to maintain a twenty-four-hour-a-day vigil until the sickness passes. Even the bowel movement of an ailing Chief Executive has been considered fit subject for a press communiqué.

Just to the right of the entrance to the White House west wing, where the President has his office, a special room has been set aside for the press, its typewriters, its telephones, its poker table. There are twenty to thirty White House "regulars" — reporters whose sole assignment is to cover this tiny beat — spend much of their day. Just across the entrance hall, the Press Secretary has offices, connected by private corridor to the President's own office. He is the hourly spokesman of the President, the constant stand-in for the public image of the Presidency. Two and three times daily he meets with the regulars and any other reporters who may wander in. These sessions may drone along on humdrum matters or just as suddenly erupt in high drama.

To the outsider there seems almost unhealthy interest in the trivial routine of the White House and its chief occupant. Throughout the day the reporters pay constant court to the Press Secretary and his assistants, checking leads, listening for tips, or simply passing the time of day. It is their consuming preoccupation to sift the heaps of ore, isolate the nuggets of news, and yearn for the quick wealth of a rich vein. Mining the news at the White House is a major industry employing a sizable body of prospectors.

But the chief event of the week occurs when the reporters, one hundred and fifty to two hundred strong, file into the ornate little room in the old State Department Building once used for signing treaties. They pack themselves row on row in tightly spaced steel folding chairs and overflow onto the rococo balcony up near the ceiling. Along the back of the room a solid bank of floodlights and cameras adds to the congestion. In the heat of Washington summer it is almost unbearable.

At the appointed hour, the doors are closed against the laggards and the nation's leading citizen hurries in from a side entrance to meet the press, figuratively wearing his several hats as head of state, chief executive, commander-in-chief, leader of his party, and the rest. He greets his audience with the habitual familiarity of one dealing with long-time intimates. His assistants march in behind him to listen but seldom to interrupt the ritual that follows.

There may be a few prepared words and then with a barely perceptible nod it begins. Reporters rise and vie for recognition. For the next half hour, the President's gaze scans the assemblage and the President's nod designates who shall be his interrogators. His choice is generally random and as a consequence the interchange of question and answer is apt to be quite haphazard. But the underlying solemnity of the occasion can never be entirely forgotten. For a time the President of the United States stands alone, unshielded by the layers of officialdom that lie between him and the public. The reporters present themselves with a reverence of manner as would intercessors before a monarch. The content of their questions, however, is not always so reverent.

The spirit of the President's press conference varies from week to week and year to year and President to President. The conference may follow a smooth and gentle course. Or it may explode with unabashed savagery, the reporters probing relentlessly into a touchy subject and the President lashing back angrily at question and questioner.

Then at a signal from the press itself, it is all over. The grand finale is a scene of frenzy. Turning their backs on the standing President, the reporters from the wire services and networks who occupy the front seats charge down the center aisle in a pushing, shoving race to reach the telephone booths just outside the door. So keen is this competition that one time a veteran correspondent broke a leg in the stampede.

Foreign visitors to the President's press conference depart from this undisciplined ritual with a feeling of awe, consternation, or outright disgust. But they rarely fail to be impressed by its importance as a central act in the high drama of American government.

Why such mutual fascination between the President and the press? What prompts the editor and publisher to devote so much money and space to the subject? And what, in turn, causes the President to put up with the incessant inroads on his privacy? No other head of government feels the obligation to suffer as great an intrusion. No other chief of state find the publicity role of the office such a continual burden.

The answer goes beyond the publisher's need for filler material to provide an offset for the advertisements. It cannot be attributed simply to the heady thrill of being in the limelight which affects most men and particularly those whose ambitions direct them toward public office. The answer lies, I submit, in the very nature of modern American government. Publicity is as essential to its orderly functioning as the power to levy taxes and pass laws.

For the President of the United States his press conference, which is his primary and most systematic effort to converse with the people on a variety of major and lesser matters, offers a challenge and an opportunity. It provides a major measure of his leadership if, as Sidney Hyman has argued in *The American President,* the distinction between "strong" and "weak" presidents can be drawn in terms of "how they manage the slippery imponderables of public opinion."

It is an awesome opportunity. As one correspondent commented about our latest President's use of the conference:

> So great is the power of the President to make news and such is the charm of the Eisenhower personality that his mood greatly influences and sometimes even dominates the national attitudes towards great events . . . Not only his state-

ments but also his expressions, his mannerisms, his humor and disposition are faithfully recorded on the TV screen and transported across the land.

Certainly, applying Hyman's concept of the President as an artist, the press conference can be regarded as the easel on which he can work with broad brush strokes. There, more regularly than in any other way, he can indicate "the problems he chooses to bring to the national attention, the time when he does it, the degree of gravity he attaches to the problem, the sense of lassitude or urgency he creates when he defines alternative solutions to it."

Any President who may lightly consider abolishing the press conference, as Eisenhower reportedly did during the hectic months before his inauguration, must come to value it as a device for keeping public attention focused on himself as the single most important person in the United States, and, for that matter, the free world. By having the floodlights thus fixed, the President can give his words and gestures subtle gradations of meaning and avoid the stark black and white they would acquire if, each time he wished to make an announcement, all the paraphernalia of publicity had to be hauled out afresh. In the press conference the President can chat with the public rather than preach to it.

There are other, more immediate audiences with whom he is communing. There is the Congress to whom he can, if he chooses, address words of intercession or exhortation which would not be altogether effective for him to speak in his weekly conferences with congressional leaders of his party. There is the vast federal bureaucracy spread out beneath him and in some ways less manageable even than the Congress. A casual word at his press conference has often broken log jams that were threatening the enactment or the administration of important programs. (A misguided word, conversely, has on occasion thrown great programs into confusion.)

There are the various organized pressure groups standing eagerly by to seize each precious utterance and use it as chisel or bludgeon with which to dislodge their programs from the rut of inattention. Finally, there are the foreign governments for whom in a time of American leadership of the free world his slightest nuance may cause untold joy or consternation. To each of these audiences and to all of them collectively, the President must address himself when he speaks to the gentlemen of the press.

There must be times, however, when the President, hearing such grandiloquent theories about his press conference, wonders if they are not a bit too finely spun. They conceal what are to him its obvious blemishes. To a large extent the conference has been shaped by the specialized needs of the press rather than by his needs.

While the President and his aides must give considerable thought to anticipating the questions that will be directed to him, he can never be altogether certain that one will not come hurtling his way catching him completely unawares. The press, not he, regulates the pattern, the flow, and, to some extent, the mood of the conference. The press even controls, within limits, its duration. It is the prerogative of the senior wire-service man to call out "Thank you, Mr. President," in order to terminate it. Those who have performed this function would doubtless argue that it is a limited power. Nevertheless, on one occasion when Merriman Smith, of the United Press, allowed the conference to run seven minutes past the customary half hour, he remarked afterward on a radio discussion program, "I understand from a high authority that the President feels we owe him that time. Well, maybe we'll pay it back next time we go to Georgia." It was a scarcely veiled hint of press displeasure over President Eisenhower's lack of contact with reporters during his vacation jaunts. There have been times too when the conference was terminated well ahead of the half hour because in the judgment of the senior wire-service man, there was news enough. Issues of great moment went unexplored that week.

For the President it is something akin to a command performance, while the various reporters may or may not attend at their individual choosing. A number of the more prominent Washington reporters and columnists rarely appear and, even among those who do, a sizable contingent have never addressed a question to the President, in this writer's observation.

The President must occasionally suffer torment as he watches the reporters seize his phrases and rush in a mad stampede to the telephones outside the conference room where, within seconds, they transform these phrases into the bulletins that create headlines all over the world.

For a brief time the President is exposed. He knows his moment of truth as clearly as any matador. Of course, he can refuse, he can evade, or he can angrily rebuff an impetuous questioner. But he must do it before curious eyes. Frequently what he does not say may prove just as newsworthy as what he does say. He must endure the stupid question and maintain his composure:

> REPORTER: Mr. President, Senator Taft at dinner last night said something about liking to talk to women reporters because they gave him an opportunity to answer questions telling them he would like to kick President Truman's teeth in. Is there any place, Mr. President, where you would like to kick him?
>
> PRESIDENT: No comment.[1]

⸙ ⸙ ⸙

> REPORTER: Mr. President, Mr. Seaborn Collins, the national commander of the American Legion, was criticized by Mountbatten, the British Lord of the Admiralty, for speak-

[1] Exchange at President Truman's Press Conference, January 4, 1951.

> ing against communism to the British Service Empire League — British Empire Service League, it is — and he said he was setting forth what the American Legion believed should be done to defeat communism and not what the United States Government thought, and he said he was not presuming to tell any other Government what to do, but it seems that Mountbatten said that this was talking about politics at a veterans meeting. I wonder if you would say what you think about the fitness of veterans everywhere considering communism as an issue of aggression. (Laughter.) [2]

He must be prepared to leap from a penetrating query about a most delicate policy matter to one about the appointment to a district judgeship, and then leap back again without growing rattled. His questioner may serve him false or misleading information on which to comment. He may suddenly find himself confronted with a diplomatic question from a foreign correspondent whose relation to his own government may be considerably less independent than is the case with American reporters:

> Joseph Chiang [of the Chinese (Nationalist) Service at the time Chinese Communist Foreign Minister Chou En-lai made a peace appeal at the Bandung Conference]: "Do you think Chinese Communists now realize America sincerely believes in peace so that she humbly came to America for help to seek peace?" [3]

There have been occasions, too, when a persistent reporter has succeeded in putting the President squarely on the spot. Take the following exchange in 1957 when President Eisenhower's Civil Rights Bill was before Congress:

> ROWLAND EVANS, JR., of the New York *Herald Tribune:* . . . Sir, are you convinced that it would be a wise extension of Federal power at this stage to permit the Attorney General

[2] Exchange at President Eisenhower's Press Conference, June 8, 1955.
[3] President's Press Conference, April 27, 1955.

to bring suits on his own motion to force school integration in the South?

PRESIDENT: Well, no; I have—as a matter of fact, as you state it that way, on his own motion, I suppose is what you are talking about—

EVANS: Yes, sir. I think that is what the bill would do, Part 3.

PRESIDENT: Well, in that we will see what they agree on . . .[4]

Those who were following the controversy realized that by a reporter's question the President had been brought face to face with a major section of legislation drafted by his deputies and had in effect repudiated it. Section three of the bill did not become law.

The President finds himself serving as an unwitting backboard against which the opinions of even the most insignificant Congressmen may be bounced so they may achieve a prominence they would never merit on their own. A large portion of the conference while Congress is in session is devoted to matters of congressional opinion. A major concern for the President is to maintain the publicity initiative which his competitors on Capitol Hill are attempting to seize from him.

He works against certain odds. Many of the reporters at his conference represent editors for whom the provincial or regional issues are more pressing than the national.

Almost as irritating to the President are the questions for which he has prepared an answer and then has not been asked. After one of Eisenhower's conferences, a White House aide listed for me six major questions involving events, policies, and programs which had gone unasked at that week's conference despite their prominence in the news. He remarked that the conferences would be considerably improved if the reporters did their homework as well as the President did. One time Eisenhower commented wryly as the

[4] President's Press Conference, July 17, 1957.

reporters trooped out of the conference room, "No one gives me an opportunity to talk about defense." The fact was that on this particular week the priorities of scandal in the White House, executions in Hungary, crisis in Lebanon took precedence over reorganization of the Defense Department even though the reorganization bill's fate was being currently decided on Capitol Hill.

Few reporters appear to devote much thought to planning their questions ahead of time. Since the President's nod of recognition usually goes to the one first on his feet, the contest often belongs to the spry limb rather than the sober brain.

Reporters differ widely in their concepts of the way the President's press conference should be conducted. There is a basic conflict of attitudes going directly to the dichotomy between the President who reigns and the President who rules — the leader who symbolizes our national purpose and the leader who is to be held accountable for the acts of his lowliest subordinates. The press uncertainly treats him first one way, then the other. At times, the President can be shamelessly evasive without having the reporters point up that fact. There have been other times, however, when they have moved in like prosecuting attorneys on a hapless criminal. One such occasion was the press conference on November 11, 1953. Reporters took President Eisenhower to task for Attorney General Brownell's speech accusing former President Truman of knowingly promoting a Communist spy in his government. From abroad, Harold Callender of the *New York Times* cabled an account of the astonished European reaction to this interrogation:

> Few would believe that the reporters would dare address the President with the challenging questions asked or that their editors published the questions and answers. No European Premier or even a foreign minister would dream of accord-

ing to the press the privileges accorded by President Eisenhower. Few European Members of Parliament and fewer reporters would venture to treat even a minor minister as American reporters treated the President.

⁄ ⁄ ⁄

The growth of the modern Presidency brought with it increased intercourse and at the same time lessened intimacy between the President and the press. The young reporter in Washington today reads with some envy about the experience of another young reporter, Henry Adams, who arrived in Washington during Andrew Johnson's Administration, later remarking: "The first step, of course, was making of acquaintance and the first acquaintance was naturally the President, to whom an aspirant to the press officially paid respect." Few reporters today ever have such personal entré to the President.

The pioneer of modern press relations was the ebullient President Theodore Roosevelt, who, according to legend, one day saw several reporters standing outside the gates of the White House interviewing departing visitors. He promptly ordered an anteroom set aside for them. Woodrow Wilson, the political scientist, believing in the value of "pitiless publicity," inaugurated the regular press conference. His ideal was to make it an interpellative device much like the question period in the British House of Commons. At the first of his conferences, eleven days after he took office, he told reporters, "A large part of the success of public affairs depends on the newspapermen — not so much the editorial writers, because we can live down what they say, as upon the news writers, because the news is the atmosphere of public affairs." But Wilson's ideal was never fulfilled. He never managed to accommodate himself to the conference's rough and tumble and in his latter days in office withdrew completely.

Warren Gamaliel Harding, a onetime newspaperman, proved exceedingly inept in dealing with the press, although one reporter of the period, Oswald Garrison Villard, has commented that "no President will ever be more carefully and more generously protected than he was." Harding's main fault lay in his indiscreet disclosures to the reporters which served to publicize his personal inadequacy. He once made a blundering interpretation of the Four Power Treaty in response to a press conference question. This created dire repercussions abroad. Thereafter the requirement was laid down that questions had to be submitted in writing in advance.

The supposedly taciturn Calvin Coolidge apparently understood well the press's compelling need for copy and utilized this need to project a public image of himself not altogether in keeping with the facts. "Silent" Cal was in reality quite vocal in his press conferences, yet on all but the most mundane matters imposed a strict rule of attribution to the mystical "White House spokesman." He surrounded the Presidency with a variety of inconsequential episodes which served to strike a warm chord in the heart of the average citizen. As Jay Hayden of the Detroit *News* noted, because Coolidge was willing to pose for almost any picture at almost any time in almost any costume, and because he was so basically colorless, the press, having a desperate need for colorful copy, manufactured the Coolidge legend. Raymond Clapper, who was United Press bureau chief at the time, wrote that "the Washington correspondents worked with their tongues in cheek."

The late Henry Suydam, then Washington correspondent for the Brooklyn *Eagle* and more recently press chief for Secretary of State Dulles, once summed it up disgustedly:

> Mr. Coolidge, with an art that almost defied description, used his press conferences for the dissemination of trivia, which, under the deft, inflating touch of correspondents, became important and significant. Mr. Coolidge would observe, with respect to a certain bill, "I'm not in favor of this legislation." The next morning Washington despatches began as follows: "President Coolidge, in fighting mood, today served notice on Congress that he intended to combat, with all the resources at his command, the pending bill, etc."

One wonders how successful Coolidge would have been in his press relations if really substantial problems had arisen to test his leadership. Certainly Herbert Hoover, who had been immensely popular with the reporters as Secretary of Commerce, found that the press conference became a wearisome burden when he moved into the Presidency and faced the dismal Depression years. Hoover's conferences were, by all accounts, sterile affairs often cited by oldtimers in the Washington press corps as the dark ages of presidential press relations. But it is noteworthy that he felt an obligation to continue them right to the bitter end of his term.

It was more than the stark contrast with his predecessor that made Franklin Roosevelt's arrival on the Washington scene seem like the age of enlightenment to the Washington correspondent. Roosevelt, as one reporter has fondly commented, was a "newspaperman's President no matter what you thought of his policies." He promptly scrapped the old rules requiring written questions and all answers attributed to a "White House spokesman." The reporters were summoned into his office on the average of twice a week and permitted to fire questions as freely as they liked. He had four categories of answers: direct quotations on special occasions, indirect quotations but with attribution to the President himself, background information that had to be written under the reporter's own authority, and off-the-record comments that could not be used at all. Roosevelt played the various categories with tremendous skill, keeping the correspondents informed even when it did not suit his purpose to inform the public. He approached the press conference with the same initiative and assuredness that he brought to the Presidency in general. He did not hesitate to deliver long lectures on economics or other matters to the hard-pressed reporters. He took delight in composing their stories for them and, many have admitted, that he had a sure eye for the news lead.

A good many newspapermen look back with nostalgia to the Roosevelt press conferences. The reporters crowded into the President's own office in those days. The laggards were obliged to stand on tiptoe to peer over the shoulders of the early arrivals so they might get a glimpse of the crippled President seated behind his desk. Despite the visual limitations, there was a spirit of informality and directness about the whole affair. The reporter shot his question at the President and received a quick retort, then hurried to get it down on the back of an envelope before the next round. There was no officially released transcript to challenge the reporter's own notations. He and he alone conveyed information about top governmental policy from the White House conference to the public. There were no short cuts except, of course, when the President took to the air to deliver one of his Fireside Chats.

Under Truman the press conference took on new formality. The President's office had long been inadequate for the large number of reporters who flocked there. In the spring of 1950, President Truman moved the conference, which he was holding weekly, from the White House to the treaty room on the fourth floor of the old State Department building next door.

Instead of being ushered into the President's presence, the

reporters were henceforth to take their seats ahead of time, whereupon he would enter from an anteroom and address them while standing behind a desk at the front of the room.

The reporters regularly rise to their feet when the President enters and remain standing until he has directed them to be seated, an act of homage they pay no one else in Washington. They identify themselves and their publications before asking their questions. The press conference has taken on aspects of a classroom seminar.

No President has enjoyed his press conferences more and none fared worse than Harry Truman. He seemed to regard them as a contest of wits between himself and the reporters. He loved to interrupt the reporters in mid-question, to taunt them jovially if they slackened the pace of the conference, to give brusque answers, and sometimes to ridicule a particular questioner, though without venom. He had a curious habit of delivering an angry retort and then breaking into a broad smile. When troubles resulted, as they sometimes did, he was wont to blame the reporters and then, when challenged by them, to pass it off as the fault of their editors and their rewrite men.

But the major fault was that Truman never was able to comprehend both the culling process of the press and the printed impact of his words. More than this, he suffered, as Joseph C. Harsch of the *Christian Science Monitor* once commented, from a habit of thinking "not consistently aware of the general implications of the specific." Harsch felt that Truman's preoccupation with the particular question being asked tended at times to confuse rather than clarify the general area of policy he was discussing.

Another weakness was that the President frequently picked up and repeated phraseology suggested by the questioner. It led to some major bloopers. Truman's famous "red herring" remark in 1948 provides a prize example of the vagaries of the conference. His statement, which returned to haunt him as a symbol of supposed "softness" toward Communist infiltration in the government, was made in answer to the following question: "Mr. President, do you think the Capitol Hill spy scare is a red herring to divert public attention from inflation?" The questioner, according to legend, was attending the President's press conference for the first time. He never came back. But certainly his phrasing of the question, which the President dutifully repeated in giving an affirmative answer, should have earned him Republican immortality.

The most celebrated press conference fiasco occurred in November 1951. The resulting news stories that the President was considering use of the atomic bomb in Korea caused repercussions throughout the world, brought Prime Minister Attlee flying to America for consultation, and, indirectly, hastened the death of the President's press secretary, Charles Ross. John Hersey has provided a masterful account of this ill-fated conference in *The New Yorker*. Having been present in the White House at the time to gather research material for a *New Yorker* profile of President Truman, Hersey was able to describe in detail the development of what was a major communications failure. The Chinese Communists had just entered the Korean War and the situation was admittedly grave. Several days before the conference a number of top United States policy planners had worked to prepare the statement which the President dutifully read at the beginning of his press conference. At no time, according to Hersey, had there been any mention of using the atomic bomb.

But Truman's prepared statement, expressing general determination to remain steadfast in the face of the new peril, was not particularly newsworthy and the reporters probed the subject for "hard" news. They got it when, in response to a question, the President affirmed that the use of the atom bomb was "always under consideration." The resulting headlines dropped the "always" and played heavily the "under consideration."

Hersey's analysis, tending to lay all the blame at the reporters' feet, could be criticized as the work of someone who was not accustomed to the routine of the press conference. The reporters could legitimately argue that there was no way for them to know what had gone on in the minds of those who had planned the President's statement. They could only assume, in the light of the President's vague intimations, that he deliberately intended to raise the specter of the atom bomb at this critical time. They could argue that by their recurrent questions — there had been five or six — they had sought to alert him to the significance of his utterances. A final definite warning had been sounded by Anthony Leviero of the *New York Times* when he asked if the President's remarks could be quoted directly. The President refused, but made no effort to clarify his remarks until after the conference when the first wire-service bulletins had already begun to spread the alarming story.

More than a specific finding of guilt, Hersey's documentary was in fact a damning indictment of the slipshodness which underlies the press conference as an institution for conveying vital information. It gave meaning to the judgment of Charles Beard, who declared that a statesman

> . . . should make his public utterances under a sense of responsibility as grave as the occasion which elicits them. The license we allow ourselves in our irresponsible moods should be put aside when we become responsible . . . I believe no President should be encouraged or forced to speak offhand on any grave question of national policy. I would have every President follow the example set by Washington and Jeffer-

> son, mature his convictions for public declaration, express them carefully, weigh his words, under the sense of responsibility that ought always to be attached to his exalted position as executive head of our nation.[5]

On the press's side, it illustrated the unspeakable folly of measuring the President's utterances with the same yardstick of newsworthiness as that used on a minor news event. It bordered on complete irresponsibility to take his words and edit them for the sensational headline and the startling lead paragraph, which was the way Mr. Truman's atom bomb remarks were handled. All the qualifying details were left out of the early bulletins. The President's remarks were shaped by the inexorable pattern of the news.

Mr. Eisenhower, both by temperament and by training, has veered in the opposite direction from Mr. Truman in his press conference practice. He steadfastly shies away from the personality conflicts which furnish the largest headlines. Matured in the practice of conducting military briefings for the politicians, he is a master at the art of saying little while talking a great deal. In apparent obedience to the Harsch doctrine, he almost automatically translates the specific into the general and shows a propensity for harking back to first principles. As one reporter commented acidly: "If you ask Ike the time of day, he will tell you all about the history of clockmaking."

President Eisenhower has had his rough moments with the press. Once, in response to persistent queries about the McCarthy forays against his Administration, he stalked angrily from the conference room. On a number of occasions, he has flushed deep red when prodded about a sensitive subject and rejected the questioner abruptly. But in the main he has

[5] Charles A. Beard, *The Republic: Conversations on Fundamentals* (New York, 1943).

achieved a gentleness in his conferences that contrasts with the flamboyance of the Truman ones. Questions involving high policy matters are asked with the broadest kind of hook on which the President can hang any answer he likes. There are dark suspicions that the partisan preferences of newspaper publishers have caused this. Certainly a more direct cause has been the fact that these are the kind of questions the President will answer.

But Eisenhower's use of the press conference has not furthered it as an instrument of lucid communication. His penchant for the vague generality as well as his willingness to comment volubly on almost any subject has tended to debase the currency value of his words. After one notable conference, a reporter observed that if the President's remarks that morning were to be taken as policy, it could be assumed: (1) that he was in conflict with his own Administration on the right and duty of public officials to state opinions on Supreme Court decisions; (2) that United States commanders in the field might or might not have authority to use atomic weapons in defense of their commands — he was not sure; (3) and that the United States might or might not wait to be attacked in a major war. There have been a number of times when the reporter would have devoutly preferred a terse "no comment" to the President's rambling soliloquy in which they could find no sense and no syntax, regardless of how much they searched.

One had the feeling, even before the television camera was introduced to the press conference, that the President was attempting to talk beyond the reporter directly to his larger audience. Though reportedly hostile to the press conference before his inauguration, he helped its further flowering. Shortly after he took office, his press secretary, James Hagerty, permitted reporters to hire a stenotypist who could produce a transcript of the conference within two or three hours for sale at a nominal fee to anyone who wanted it. The *New York Times* promptly began printing the transcript regularly. The requirement that the President be recorded only in the third person lost a great deal of its validity, since anyone could easily figure out exactly what he had said simply by changing "he" to "I" and making appropriate changes in syntax. It put an added premium on the President's preciseness in expressing himself since it created an accurate file of his statements from week to week. Malapropisms could no longer be attributed to faulty reporting.

To accommodate radio correspondents, Mr. Hagerty began to release large sections of the transcript for direct quotation, thus permitting tape recordings of the President's voice to be broadcast. The entry of the television and movie news cameras into the conference room in January of 1955 was one more step in the process of extending the press conference. Its actual timing was determined in large part by the development of the remarkably fast Eastman Tri-X film, which eliminated the necessity of great numbers of klieg lights. It had been the lights more than the cameras that had concerned Press Secretary Hagerty.

For some gloomy critics this latest development has been the last straw, the final debasement of the conference as a profitable opportunity for communication with the President. Assuming that the reporter can get himself recognized, his question and the accompanying answer are formally transcribed, recorded, taped, and filmed. Almost before he can file his own copy both he and the President have been viewed on television screens all across the country. He has become, say these critics, an unpaid extra in a gigantic show. He has sold his birthright for a mess of publicity.

Those who hold the contrary view stress the effect of these

innovations in improving this important institution of government. By accommodating all the mass media, the President can more easily communicate with the citizenry. The press conference was never meant to be simply a special preserve for reporters. The camera has as much right in the room as the reporter himself. To him still belongs the job of weighing and comparing, and of developing the whole story — a responsibility he was prone to duck when he served as the exclusive conduit of news. Now that he is less a mere recorder, he can become a more creative interpreter.

✓ ✓ ✓

President Truman at his press conference was the backwoods Baptist laying down a personal testament of God and Mammon to the congregated reporters. President Eisenhower has preferred to be the high priest, whose utterances contain less fire and more theology. He has been more successful in conducting his press relations without the damaging flare-ups that marked the Truman era. Only on very rare occasions has he been obliged to issue a post-conference "clarification."

Yet, for both the latest two Presidents, the press conference has been in a deeper sense a failure. For Truman it produced an impression of presidential arrogance and obstinacy that worsened his working relations with Congress and reduced his appeal to all but the most partisan public. Eisenhower, on the other hand, has conveyed through it an impression of irresolution. He has maintained the image of the President who reigns, but there has been a blurring of the image of the President who rules, of the leader who stands for specific issues and against specific issues, who likes certain people and, yes, hates certain people. He has kept his conferences calm and casual. "What everybody does not know," James Reston has written about one Eisenhower conference, "is just how far this habit of casual or inaccurate official talk, inflated by the modern techniques of public relations, propaganda, and mass communications, has added to the political confusion and cynicism of our time."

It can be argued that in both Truman's and Eisenhower's cases the failure of the press conference has been merely symptomatic of more fundamental failures of leadership. From personal observation, however, I believe it has tended to aggravate their problems. It has compounded the difficulty of leadership for the President in an era when he deals with issues incapable of easy or quick solution.

The President's press conferences have not contributed the way they should to the formation of a truly enlightened public opinion. As Zechariah Chafee has noted, "They tempt a President to blurt out anything that boils up in his emotions and do his thinking out loud in public." There are times when the thoughtful onlooker is dumfounded by the offhand manner in which unmatured convictions on critically grave issues are voiced by the nation's Chief Executive. The difficulties provoked by this practice are not lessened now that the President's every word becomes a part of historic record.

Quite a few people have critically examined the shortcomings of the President's press conference. By and large they fall into two groups: the abolitionists and the reformers. The abolitionists, who include a Supreme Court Justice in their ranks, claim that the conference is one of the worst abuses in a capital where publicity has become a policy in itself rather than a product of policy. It involves the President in a vicious circle, utterly disrupting the consistent, reasoned growth of policy. And it demands of him a superhuman degree of restraint and wisdom.

A telling riposte to the abolitionists was voiced by one

veteran Washington correspondent: "Okay, cut out the President's press conferences — better cut out the Secretary of State's and the other Cabinet officers' while you're at it. Then let the Administration enemies on the Hill dominate the headlines!" His answer reveals the extent to which the need for publicity must be a dominating concern among those responsible for executive leadership in America.

Those who offer various proposals for reform of the President's press conference include a number of prominent newspapermen. James Reston has written, "The Presidential press conference, like most of our political institutions today, has not kept pace with the changing requirements of the times. It was started in the days of the Model T, and is now trying to operate unchanged in the age of the Jupiter C. In fact, if anything, it has become more open and casual as the elements of accident, danger and risk have increased."

The remedy, Reston says, "is simply to modify the present procedure so as to protect the President while preserving the spontaneity of a useful and uniquely American institution." Exactly how to accomplish this, however, is not so simple. A number of minor changes have been suggested to channel the wild torrents of the conference, including: more systematic preparatory briefing; active participation by the President's advisers, especially when they sense something going wrong; a brief post conference session conducted by the Press Secretary to clear up possible misunderstandings; and a delayed release time on publication of conference news.

Like most practicing newspapermen, Reston is strongly opposed to a return to the requirement of submitting written questions in advance — a practice which evokes memories of the stultifying conferences of Harding and Hoover. Instead, he suggests that in response to certain difficult questions the President promise to provide studied answers in writing later in the week. With a newspaperman's shrewdness, he points out that this practice would lighten the burden imposed on understaffed Washington news bureaus, which can hardly do justice in a single day to the great variety of questions and answers presently evoked at the press conference. The President would thus reap the benefit of providing "more front page copy on more days of the week."

In much of the discussion on this subject there is the inherent suspicion that any tampering with the President's press relations will inevitably lead to a form of propaganda dictatorship. According to one direful prediction, the day is not far distant when the President will have his own television theater instead of the present antiquated conference room. "There will be . . . nothing to prevent the President from having a press conference a day, if he likes, and flooding the television screens with prepared answers to questions written in advance. Thus, while the other 'equal' branch of the Government, Congress, is arguing its case to virtually empty seats, the President would be in a position to use the carefully prepared and televised conference to overwhelm the weaker voice of Congress."

It is, of course, possible that a future demagogue in the White House might find ways to dominate the channels of communication in America. But the more immediate danger, in my opinion, lies in the inadequate means by which the President can communicate responsibly and responsively with the people. The more immediate need is to provide him a rigorous challenge — one that he cannot ignore or evade — to keep the public informed.

This is not to say that there must be more publicity gimmicks for artificially stimulating the public curiosity about their Chief Executive. I am convinced that useful limits have already been passed in the effort to project an image of the President as a human being who disports himself very much like everyone else. What is needed, and what the President should take care to project, is the image of a leader who governs. The primary function of his press relations should be to keep him in constant contact with the needs and anxieties of the people and to permit him to respond with clear and reasoned judgments.

3

The Publicity Powers of Congress

> Nothing affects more the balance of power between Congress and the President than whether the one or the other is the principal source of news and explanation and opinion.
>
> WALTER LIPPMANN

THE MEMBER OF CONGRESS is uniquely creator and creature of publicity. It is the nature of his job to be concerned with that amorphous substance known as public opinion, and with the processes by which the public attention is attracted and public opinion shaped. He lives in a state of intimacy with the newspaperman baffling to outsiders who mistake this vital relationship for pure cronyism. He employs his highest-paid assistant to diagnose and fill the prescriptive needs of the press. For the lone Congressman, the ideal is so to affect his press relations that back in his constituency the news is ever presented on a "me and the President" basis. The more ambitious members seek to extend the constituency to which this image is projected.

The individual publicity drive of the Congressman may seem a minor and unimportant phenomenon. Collectively, reinforced by the publicity-making mechanisms of the congressional committees, it gives a congressional bias to the news which creates certain advantages for the Legislative

Branch of government in its continuing power struggle with the Executive. It contributes at times to a constitutional imbalance that seems to be a recurrent disorder in American government.

The press is omnipresent on the Hill. Just over the presiding officer's desk in each House hovers the Press Gallery, its occupants constantly monitoring the proceedings and frequently outnumbering the legislators present on the floor below. For the wire services there are special muted telephones within the chamber itself, ready for the instant communiqué about a critical congressional action.

Behind swinging doors off the gallery, the press has its quarters for work and relaxation with staff assistants paid for by the Congress. Teletypes stand ready to relay copy to the great central offices of the wire services. The walls are lined with the typewriters and the telephone booths essential to the business. Great leather couches offer all-night accommodation should the legislative session drag on. In nearby studios the reporters for radio and television can originate their broadcasts and interview their captive Congressmen. Room for the ever expanding needs of the press has been carved out of strange nooks and crannies in the ancient Capitol building.

The congressional Press Galleries have the largest membership of accredited reporters in Washington, several times the size of the White House Correspondents' Association. Their membership cards are generally accepted as suitable accreditation for official functions even outside the jurisdiction of Congress — a minor but not insignificant symptom of congressional paramountcy in the organization of Washington press relations.

When Congress is in session, Capitol Hill becomes a mecca for large numbers of the press. The syndicated columnist and the reporter for the provincial paper hurry along the long corridors to the committee sessions or crowd into the congested press conferences called by the legislative potentates. Day after day the bulk of the news that flows out of Washington is congressional-oriented.

⸙ ⸙ ⸙

Despite the absence of powerful national newspapers during the early years of the republic, the press found much more ready acceptance in covering the business of the American Congress than was the case with the British Parliament. In the House of Commons, the presence of reporters in the visitors' galleries was jealously resisted until well into the nineteenth century. Even today the reporter can be technically evicted from the gallery by a Member's cry "I spy a stranger!" — though in actual practice this no longer occurs.

In the House of Representatives, the presence of the editor–letter writer, precursor of the modern correspondent, was accepted from the beginning. At first the Senate kept its doors closed — to House members as well as reporters. This initial exclusion was thought to be one reason why the Senate during its early years was always considered the lesser of the two "coequal" chambers. (Today, interestingly, the more newsworthy character of Senate deliberations plays no small part in creating the public assumption that it is the superior body.)

The Senators soon relented and invited in reporters. When Congress moved to Washington in 1800, it was discovered that the viewers' gallery in the Senate was too far removed for the reporters to be able to keep up with what was going on below. As a result they were invited down to the floor, where they were given a privileged position at the feet of the Vice-President. It was many years before the Executive Branch thought to arrange comparable facilities for the reporting of its operations.

An early congressional attempt to discipline the press after the British method — by summoning the offending journalist before the bar of the Senate — came to naught. The newspaperman William Duane, of the *Aurora,* who had reputedly written articles tending "to defame the Senate of the United States," simply declined to accept the summons. The Senators, with the supporting vote of Vice-President Thomas Jefferson, voted Duane guilty of contempt and charged the Sergeant-at-Arms to take him into custody. But as one early historian has recorded: "Just then Mr. Duane had business out of town too urgent to be neglected or else the Senate became conscious that it had overstepped its bounds; at any rate there was no arrest." More recently, Congress has altogether ceased the practice of holding its own contempt proceedings, but instead turns its grievances over to the Justice Department for prosecution in the courts.

There were indeed early Congressmen, enraged by cavalier treatment they had received at the hand of the reporters, who uttered the fateful curse that they might be rid of them. History records that time after time these recalcitrant members were soon beseeching the press to lift its boycott. On occasion, a reporter was temporarily evicted. There was the sad case of Congressman Sawyer of Ohio, who in the late 1840's was held up to ridicule by a New York *Tribune* reporter for bringing his lunch of bologna sausage and crackers to the House Chamber where he ate it behind the Speaker's desk, later wiping his hands on his bald head and picking his teeth with his jackknife. As a consequence, the New York *Tribune* reporters were barred from the chamber for a time. But ever after the poor Congressman was known among his colleagues as "Sausage Sawyer."

For the most part, Congressmen quite early recognized the

importance of good relations with the press and made the best of it. Some even turned it to financial profit. One Speaker of the House, a voluble gentleman, once boasted that he averaged $100 a week selling news and complained that being inexperienced for a long time, he had allowed himself to be interviewed for nothing.

Such commercialism is not so blatant nowadays, although it is by no means uncommon for the member of Congress to synchronize his publicity drives with highly profitable articles in the magazines and appearances on the lecture platform. A White House aide once confided to reporters that for President Eisenhower to denounce Senator McCarthy publicly would only double the fee the Senator could command. It was a cynical way of expressing the dilemma of dealing with a figure whose principal item in trade was publicity.

In the United States Congress, the reporter is no longer barred, except from certain committee meetings. His access to individual legislators is frequent and intimate. Near each chamber there are private rooms to which the members are willingly summoned in a never ending file for communion with the press. During a lively session the President's Room just off the Senate lobby is continuously crowded with little clusters of solons and scribes, two by two, exchanging earnest confidences. Special doormen stand ready at the request of correspondents to call still others away from the debate. At times this little anteroom contains more Senators than the Senate Chamber. The creation of the public image of the debate is more engrossing to most of them than the actual debate itself.

A few steps inside the Senators' lobby, a battery of tickers brings back the news minutes after it is dispatched. Nowhere else in Washington does one more keenly sense the cyclical movement of policy and publicity. Across the Capitol, a similar drama is being enacted in the House of Representatives. There, even the members' lobby is open to the prowling correspondent.

Even the fledgling correspondent in Washington finds an ease of access to congressional leaders which makes Congress for him a happy hunting ground of journalistic enterprise. The senior reporters assigned to the Hill share an intimacy with these leaders which lesser members of Congress seldom gain. At least once daily the wire-service representatives are invited in for sessions with the Speaker of the House and the Senate Majority Leader. On countless unnamed occasions the reporter may attend the informal convocations at which the earthier matters of politics are explored. Not infrequently he is a direct participant in the act of legislative policy making, a privilege he would hardly be accorded in the Executive departments.

There is good reason for his prerogatives. The play of the news helps to regulate the orderly flow of legislative business, or, alternatively, to thrust an unaccounted item out of the darkness of committee neglect into the limelight of full congressional attention. It stirs mutinies among the rank-and-file Congressmen or squelches them. The pressures of publicity can reinforce the unspecified Constitutional authority of the potentates on the Hill when they seek to pit their power against the Executive. Access to the news writers provides the Congressman a chance to contribute his interpretation to the first draft of history, which he hopes will in turn help shape the course history takes.

At times the raw competition to service the press takes on bizarre proportions. The following account appeared in a "Footnote to the News" column of the Washington *Post and Times-Herald:*

> A freshman Senator outslicked his veteran colleagues to pick off the easiest publicity plum available last week. He was Clifford P. Case (R-N. J.), whose reaction comment to the

> President's decision [to veto the Natural Gas Bill] was the first to hit the Senate press gallery. His prize was a prominent play in the afternoon newspapers.
>
> Behind his speed was the quick thinking and faster legs of Sam Zagoria, Case's administrative assistant and former Washington Post and Times-Herald reporter.
>
> Zagoria had run off several copies of the Senator's "isn't-it-grand" statement early Wednesday morning. He then parked himself by the Associated Press teletype in the Senate lobby. When the flash came through, he hightailed it back to the press gallery, one floor above, where eager reporters were waiting to write reaction accounts. Zagoria beat a runner for Sen. William A. Purtell (R-Conn.) by one minute flat.

On an average day the long table in the Senate Press Gallery is littered with the mimeographed news releases from the Senators. This predigested copy summarizes their views on every conceivable issue, domestic and foreign. The American legislator, uniquely among the parliamentarians of the world, is sensitively alert to the business of systematic press relations.

For the reporter, it is more than easy access which makes Congress a primary news source. The business of Congress is the stuff of which good news reporting is made. Congress is a continuing scene of drama and conflict and intrigue. Its battles can be described in terms of colorful personalities rather than amorphous issues that may confound the copy desk and confuse the reader. Washington is a highly fragmented capital city in which it is not always simple for the reporter to follow the thread of his story. But it is possible for him to glimpse the image of the total story in the congressional mirror, indeed, to see its outlines in a bold relief that may not be so apparent on direct view.

Perhaps inevitably there should be this "congressional bias" to the news. There is, in addition, a degree of protectionism that comes into play. Powerful pressures dissuade the reporter from being as zealous an exposer of Congress itself as he is of the Executive departments. His stock in trade in terms of news "exclusives" depends upon the preservation of a chummy relationship with members of Congress. A great amount of news is dispensed to him as a favor and must be regarded as such. There is not quite the same camaraderie about news gathering in the more austere precincts of the Executive.

On the other hand, the retaliation for unfavorable publicity can be much swifter and more vengeful from Congress. It is by no means unusual for a member, enraged by something appearing in print, to take to the floor in a violent attack against the offending reporter. Such is the clublike atmosphere of the two houses, that no member is likely to come to the reporter's defense. Abuse of the most vicious sort has been heaped on the head of the offending journalist while the Senators and the galleries listened in uneasy silence.

On April 10, 1950, Senator Harry Cain rose on the Senate floor to answer an assertion by *Time* Magazine that he was among the Senate's "expendables." For the better part of the afternoon he centered an attack on *Time*'s congressional correspondent. "If ever I sat with a human being who was smug, arrogant, self-centered, vain and frustrated . . . This ulcer-burdened young American who could neither vote nor fight . . . The agent *Time* Magazine has today was a 4-F in peace . . . has undoubtedly encouraged other men to die, but he has never stood on the sidelines and watched them die.

"During our conversation," Cain concluded, "I lost the rich anger and indignation which has possessed me for several weeks. I lost even what had been my desire to laugh in the face of this pygmy. I did not even want to bat him around physically because that would have been like punching a bag of mush."

Not one Senator remonstrated against this disgusting tirade.

As one who has had the experience of being thus attacked by a senior Senator, this reporter can testify to the unpleasantness of the experience. Only after several efforts was it possible to find one of his colleagues willing to insert a factual reply in the *Congressional Record.* Privately, many were ready to vouchsafe their sympathies.

The reporter knows there is slim likelihood of any follow-up on his initiative should he publish evidence of corruption or wrongdoing on the Hill. For one who turns up malfeasance in the Executive Branch, there is always a congressional committee standing by eager to pick up and pursue the matter. In fact, the publication of the exposé and the commencement of the committee probe have sometimes been carefully coordinated in advance. Reporter and committee counsel work hand in glove to reap its full benefits. But Congressmen are seldom as prone to examine one another. Nor is the Executive Branch always alert to bear down on congressional abuses. It has no publicity mechanisms comparable to the congressional committee probe for airing such abuses.

I do not mean to imply there is a preponderance of virtue in the Executive Branch or of vice in the Legislative, but merely to point out that the publicity processes do not provide so strict a surveillance of the latter. There are countless instances when Congressmen demand special privilege that would provoke great furor if made by an administration official. The legislator moves in an area of protectionism that extends even to his unwise public utterances. Members of the press often apply a deliberate censorship. One neophyte reporter who unwittingly quoted in print a rash remark revealing bigotry on the part of a leading Congressman told me he was afterward chastised by several of his press colleagues for this indiscretion.

Women correspondents covering Capitol Hill circulate

among themselves the names of those members of Congress with whom it is unsafe to be alone. One or two solons have been known to be real sex reprobates. But no word of their misdemeanors ever reaches the reading public. Senators have been seen to stagger drunkenly onto the Senate floor and deliver unintelligible harangues without creating a ripple in the press. Considering the great glare of publicity that beats down on Congress, the unillumined corners are the more curious.

This protectionism even covers some of the collective activities in Congress. Year in and year out minor frauds on public understanding are committed without being duly noted by the press. Each year, for example, the House Appropriations Committee or one of its subcommittees virtuously makes deep cuts in appropriations bills for funds already contractually obligated. Each year, this action is duly rewarded by newspaper accounts that the Committee has "slashed" the budget by such and such an amount. And later each year the Committee quietly restores the cut in its "supplemental" appropriations. Yet, one reporter told me, though tempted he wouldn't dare lead his story with the fact that "the congressmen have made this cut with the full expectation, as in former years, of restoring it later in the Session when the public isn't looking."

⁊ ⁊ ⁊

Amid the publicity drives of Congress the investigative committee exerts the most powerful thrust. It is geared to the production of headlines on a daily and even twice daily basis. It is able to create the news story which lingers week after week on the front pages to form an indelible impression on the public mind. No institution of the Executive Branch is capable of such sustained and well-manipulated publicity.

It is a bewildering discovery for the newcomer to Capitol Hill to come upon the publicity trapping of the congressional probe. Within the marble conference rooms of the dignified old congressional buildings, the technicians of the mass media have taken over. Row on row of reporters occupy the forward seats. Crouching directly before the beleaguered witness are the still photographers, ever ready to thrust their cameras into his face to record each symptom of anger, grief, or perhaps only confusion caused by the noise and fuss. In the Senate committees a backdrop of klieg lights and TV and movie cameras completes the stage setting for this bizarre function claimed to be part of the "legislative process." The House has recently prohibited the presence of television and movie cameras because of the antiquarian publicity notions of the Speaker.

One witness who was questioned for more than ten hours before a committee has put down his recollections of that event:

> The physical setup a witness faces is most disconcerting . . . There were, I think, seven microphones or recording devices in front of me, so placed that it was impossible to have my papers before me in any way that gave easy access to the documents . . . The bright lights necessary for television were shining in my eyes all the time they were on, throughout the day. It meant that when I lifted my eyes to look toward committee members, I was almost blinded. It was extremely difficult to read from documents . . .[1]

The startling thing is that the committee members accept this intrusion of the image makers without question. Only the rare committee chairman ever attempts to impose limits on what the press can do. Committee members don sun glasses to protect themselves against the klieg-light glare and endure unprotestingly the heat and clamor. Even

[1] G. Bromley Oxnam, *I Protest* (New York, 1954). An account of the hearing before the House Un-American Activities Committee, July 21, 1953.

during the celebrated MacArthur hearings, affected by highest military security at a time of war in Korea, the compulsion to accommodate the press was overriding. Teams of stenotypists and mimeographers fed to the waiting reporters a fast-moving stream of verbal transcription of the witnesses' testimony read and cleared in haste by a military censor. It was as if the business of the nation would come to a halt unless the latest word was served up to the waiting public.

The most notable committee investigations are seldom in point of fact "investigations." They are planned deliberately to move from a preconceived idea to a predetermined conclusion. The skill and resourcefulness of the chairman and a sizable staff are pitted against any effort to alter its destined course. Whatever investigating is done takes place well in advance of the public hearing. The hearing is the final act in the drama. Its intent, by the staging of an arresting spectacle, is to attract public attention, to alarm or to allay, to enlighten, or, yes, sometimes to obscure.

In 1943, the counsel of a House committee investigating the Federal Communications Commission distributed a confidential memorandum to Committee members which inadvertently fell into the hands of outsiders. It had been prepared for the Committee by a reporter for International News Service, whose talents later carried him high in the employ of the Republican National Committee. Its seven points remain a classic disquisition on the publicity requirements for an "investigation":

> 1. Decide what you want the newspapers to hit hardest and then shape each hearing so that the main point becomes the vortex of the testimony. Once that vortex is reached, *adjourn.*
>
> 2. In handling press releases, first put a release date on them, reading something like this: "For release at 10:00 A.M. EST July 6," etc. If you do this, you can give releases out as

much as 24 hours in advance, thus enabling reporters to study them and write better stories.

3. Limit the number of people authorized to speak for the committee, to give out press releases or to provide the press with information to the *fewest number possible.* It plugs leaks and helps preserve the concentration of purpose.

4. Do not permit distractions to occur, such as extraneous fusses with would-be witnesses, which might provide news that would bury the testimony which you want featured.

5. Do not space hearings more than 24 or 48 hours apart when on a controversial subject. This gives the opposition too much opportunity to make all kind of counter-charges and replies by issuing statements to the newspapers.

6. Don't ever be afraid to recess a hearing even for five minutes, so that you keep the proceedings completely in control so far as creating news is concerned.

7. *And this is most important:* don't let the hearings or the evidence ever descend to the plane of a personal fight between the Committee Chairman and the head of the agency being investigated. The high plane of a duly-authorized Committee of the House of Representatives *examining* the operations of an Agency of the Executive Branch for constructive purposes should be maintained at all costs.

The memo furnishes blatant evidence of the extent to which publicity considerations can mold the committee investigation. The allusion in point 5 to "the opposition" simply means those who are being investigated. It is a rare investigation, and certainly a poorly publicized one, which has not passed judgment on the "opposition" long before the hearings.

Publicity is frequently the end product and not the sideline of the committee's work. In some of the more notable probes the final committee conclusions have been a matter of scant importance. After two particularly sensational ones of recent years — the MacArthur dismissal inquiry and the

Army-McCarthy hearings — the chairmen sought to dispense with the formality of a report altogether, each making vague assertions that the public had "the facts" and could form its own judgments. The responsibility to come up with remedial legislation is often forgotten in the shuffle. The cleansing power of publicity is considered remedy enough.

No one can seriously dispute the usefulness of the congressional committee investigation. As Senator J. William Fulbright has declared, "It provides the legislative branch with eyes and ears and a thinking mechanism." Over the past four decades, as investigations grew into a major activity of Congress, it is possible to outline an impressive record of the looking, listening, and cogitating that Congress has accomplished through its committees.

But it also provides the Legislative Branch with a broadcasting mechanism. Here many of the dilemmas of the investigating committee arise. Much committee practice that would cause little concern if conducted only before the limited audience of Congress provokes tremendous concern when it is enacted on a floodlit national stage, observed by millions.

In his book *Grand Inquest,* Telford Taylor has pointed out that the modern committee investigation with all its publicity fanfare was developed with the active connivance of the Executive Branch of the government. "Observing the immense success, both psychological, and legislative, of the Pecora hearings," he wrote, "the leaders of the Roosevelt Administration rightly concluded that investigations were unsurpassed as a means of formulating and awakening public support for the governmental measures they had in mind."

It is ironic that these leaders did not foresee the inherent dangers in committee probes conducted for the most part by senior members of Congress holding scant loyalty to the Administration in power. Before very long, the congressional investigation had been effectively turned into a means for "formulating and awakening" public opposition to the Administration and its measures. Commencing in 1939 with the Dies Committee of the House of Representatives and continuing right up to the present, the committee probe has been a formidable weapon in the hands of powerful individuals and groups in Congress seeking to dissipate popular support for the Executive Branch. In an age of big government, it has proved a more effective weapon at times than the power of the purse string or the purely law-making powers of Congress.

It is not surprising that this should be so. The investigating committee, unhampered by the need for a clear definition of purpose, guided by the flimsiest rules of procedure and relevancy, its leadership not necessarily representative of prevailing opinion in Congress and not subject to review for its misdeeds, has nearly unlimited discretion. It can stage the kind of spectacle that will produce news and attract public attention.

With the steady build-up of the public image of the chairman and certain key members, cast in their half judge, half prosecutor role, there develops what Telford Taylor calls "the illusion of investigative omnipotence." The committee decides which witnesses and facts are considered relevant to public opinion and in what order of priority. Against this, an illusion of Executive incompetence can be created as day after day the accusations are called forth at a rate which no dreary recital of the answering facts can hope to match. In the battle for the headlines the rebuttal can hardly compete if it cannot be summarized in a few catchy words.

But the illusion extends still farther. At one point or another many of these investigations founder on the rock of what is called "executive privilege." Since Congress has devised no way to test the constitutional limits of its right to probe the executive and the courts are notably reluctant to arbitrate, the conflict goes unresolved. But in the testing before the court of public opinion, it is always Congress that casts itself in the role of judge, conveniently forgetting its role as plaintiff. The Army-McCarthy hearings, for example, dealt, as one knowledgeable observer put it, with "the basic constitutional problems of the correct relationship between the two main branches of the American government." Yet, the hearings were conducted by the same investigative subcommittee which had been a party to the dispute. Only Chairman McCarthy temporarily stepped down.

These celebrated hearings remain a landmark of publicity gone riot. Day after day for two months the testimony was carried *in toto* to the waiting television public. A great department of the government was kept in a state of suspension while its leaders were made to perform in the congressionally staged drama.

Reporters who have sat through countless hours of these investigations can vouchsafe how difficult it is for a witness to overcome the enormous publicity advantage of the biased committee. Of course, memorable exceptions have occurred. In 1947 the flamboyant Howard Hughes, aided by a skilled public relations man, succeeded in igniting backfires of publicity that forced his inept inquisitor, Senator Owen Brewster, to retreat. More recently, there was a similar attempt by a witness to play directly to press and public when the House Special Subcommittee on Legislative Oversight began to probe the affairs of New England tycoon Bernard Goldfine and particularly his dealings with the Assistant to the President, Sherman Adams. Goldfine, accompanied by a retinue of lawyers and publicity agents, set up headquarters in a Washington hotel, staged press and television conferences day and night, timed releases to compete with committee-inspired headlines, and pursued a calculated public relations policy to make himself appear, as one aide put it, "a simple, innocent, underdog type being persecuted by a powerful congressional subcommittee." The efforts reached a climax at a hastily summoned midnight press conference in Goldfine's suite. In the course of it, one of Goldfine's agents fished a microphone out from under a doorway to an adjoining room. A committee investigator and a reporter secreted in the next room had been "bugging" their private conversations.

Philip Deane, of the London *Observer,* cabled his English readers a graphic account of his visit to the Goldfine publicity headquarters:

> We were shushed into silence while the television news was switched on. One of the well-known commentators was speaking of the latest developments in the Goldfine case. When mentioning Goldfine himself, the television star lost control and an Homeric laugh spread across his distinguished face . . .
>
> "Great! Great!" said Mr. Jack Lotto, Public Relations Counsellor to the Goldfine interests. "That's what we want; we want people to laugh."
>
> "Please," said a European journalist, earnestly puzzled, "did you say you wanted people to laugh at your employer?" . . .
>
> "It's like this," explained a fellow journalist. "When McCarthy attacked Senator Millard Tydings, of Maryland, Tydings tried to defend himself with dignity and failed miserably. His Public Relations firm made a fascinating study of this and decided that the only way to fight an attack by Congressional investigation is to raise more noise than your opponent, make the whole thing into a farce."

> "People don't think of you as a villain when they are laughing at you," said Mr. Williamson thoughtfully.
>
> "Doesn't Goldfine mind being made a clown?" asked the European.
>
> "You're thinking in terms of your own country. People here are different," said the American journalist. "Actually, there's a good deal of sympathy for Goldfine. He has done less than most business men do. He gives vicuña coats. Others give mistresses to married men. Have you seen salesmen entertaining buyers at Las Vegas?
>
> "This is sad because Goldfine is cute and he is not such a bad example of the great American dream—poor immigrant boy makes good. Lotto here is applying the conclusions of the Tydings case, defending the Goldfine integrity by destroying the Goldfine dignity while incidentally, the whole United States Administration goes down gloriously in a cloud of fudge."

The net effect of this and similar publicity brouhahas has been to divert the public's attention from the underlying ills in government which need legislative attention. Amid the aimless airing of charges, the quest reduces itself to a confused chase after individual villains rather than a purposeful inquiry to get at the root causes and to devise lasting solutions.

The proliferation of publicity-inspired investigations has taken us in the direction of what might be called the mass media mandate. Decisions tend to be taken not in an orderly, procedural way but on the basis of what is instantly explainable through the mass media to the public. The trouble is that a great many of the complex issues of our time are not susceptible to this kind of explanation. To attempt to do so only serves to distract government from its more important tasks and to burden the public with choices it is not equipped to make. It opens the way for the demagogue who is prepared to oversimplify the grave issues of our time and to regard publicity as an end rather than a means in the drive for power.

⸙ ⸙ ⸙

The American politician has always been something of a dramatist in search of an audience, more flamboyant, a greater individualist than his European counterpart. Cause for his behaviorisms can be traced back through the loose party system to the free enterprising traditions of American politics. More recently, however, there has begun to emerge in the halls of Congress a new type of politician conditioned to the age of the mass media and more keenly aware of the uses of publicity. He is not apt to be a member of what William S. White calls the "Inner Club," where emphasis is still put on seniority and skill in negotiation. He need not be in the forefront among those who uphold the ancient traditions of eloquence in congressional debate. Nor need he be assiduous in preparing legislation and attending to the thousand and one chores of pushing it through to enactment.

Rather he is a man versed in the subtleties of appealing beyond Congress directly to the mass audience. He knows the formula of the news release, the timing, the spoon-feeding necessities of the publicity drive. He assesses with a canny shrewdness the areas of enterprise that will best lend themselves to a sustained publicity build-up. He is an artist at stealing the Monday morning headlines with the Sunday afternoon television interview, twice gleaning the harvest of a single effort. He may be actually quite unindustrious, but he is an expert at skimming the cream of public attention while eschewing the thin milk of legislative drudgery. He is a master at shadow play, creating the illusion of magnificent drama from a reality that may be quite mundane. Usually he is lacking in direct influence among his colleagues.

But he acquires a special standing commensurate with his reflected power as a "nationally known" figure.

To more or less degree every politician who makes his way in Congress today must have something of this new sense. Even one like Senator Russell, the arch prototype of traditionalism, can be lured from the sanctity of the Senate cloakroom to dab on the makeup powder and endure the TV director's shouts of "Take one . . . take two." But it is possible to isolate advanced specimens of this genus *politicus* for whom publicity has been a more durable stock in trade than seniority or legislative prestige. Among these I would include Richard Nixon, Republican, who was catapulted to national prominence and power — from newly elected Congressman to Vice-President — in the brief span of six years without having his name tied to a single notable legislative achievement except the exposure of Alger Hiss.

"The Vice-President is a unique official of government," Nixon declared not long ago. "He has access to information in all areas but power in none." This appraisal only tells the half of it. For the advent of Richard M. Nixon to the Vice-Presidency has brought a remarkable transformation to this ancient burial chamber for politicians. Traditionally, the Vice-President has had limited alternatives. He could disappear Throttlebottom-like from public view. He could achieve a certain prominence by his stubborn antagonism to the President, as in the case of Jack Garner. He could use the office to pursue pet projects the way Henry Wallace did. He could become a traveling promoter of good causes in the fashion of Alben Barkley.

But Nixon's arrival in the Vice-Presidency coincided with the full flowering of television, and he has applied many of TV's techniques to develop the potential of his office. He has demonstrated that the Vice-President, if he is skillful, can manipulate the fade-in and the fade-out, the filters and the cropping devices familiar to the cinematographer. In times of crisis, he can even employ television's technique of "going to black" — that is, he can remove the image from the screen altogether for a calculated interval.

Willian S. White has remarked on this same phenomenon: "[Nixon's] curiously sheltered position — deeply in the Administration but not necessarily or always *of* it, and not directly accountable either to it or for its decisions — has meant that most of his actions have been made known on a leaked or ex-parte basis." It is precisely in this area of journalism by leak that the press in Washington is most vulnerable. The reporter made privy to a confidence feels bound to extract every last ounce of publicity value from it. The same trifling anecdote can ricochet around town, gathering momentum as it moves from news item to Sunday feature page to full-dress magazine article.

Also to be included high on this list of the new politician is Senator Estes Kefauver, Democrat, who has been regularly rejected by his more powerful colleagues from membership in the Inner Club but stands as the very symbol of Senator for countless Americans. Kefauver, while deliberately spurning the conventional steps to senatorial success, has come closer than any of his colleagues since Warren G. Harding in 1920 to gaining the Presidential nomination while still a member of that body. A quiet-spoken, not particularly eloquent man, he scarcely fits the picture of the new-type politician. But his crime investigations in 1950, among the first to introduce the television camera into the committee room, showed his precocity. He had a genius for publicity creation. One of the minor dramas on Capitol Hill has been the feverish maneuvering of his jealous colleagues to prevent Kefauver from ever again striking such a rich publicity bonanza.

As reporters who have worked closely with him can testify, he shows an uncanny knack for lifting an idea or an issue out of the trough of neglect and placing it squarely on page one. On one occasion during the celebrated Dixon-Yates controversy, Kefauver exposed with resounding headline clatter the name of a Budget Bureau official who was reputedly a culprit in the attempt to sabotage the Tennessee Valley Authority. It turned out that the same man had been named months earlier by Senator Lister Hill, a more traditional politician without the flair for publicity. No one had noticed.

The career of Senator Joseph McCarthy has demonstrated the capacity of this new force to be used in the cause of pure demagoguery. McCarthy represented something quite new in the history of the American demagogue. The traditional demagogue could be measured by how skillfully he sized up and played on fears and prejudices existing in a region or within a social group. McCarthy's skill, on the other hand, lay primarily in his capacity to stage a single issue so as to dominate the channels of communication and to distract a national audience. Alongside Huey Long or Tom Heflin he would have cut a poor figure in poise and personality. But they would probably have fared badly by comparison with him in the sure mastery of the ways to manipulate the mass media. They knew how to sway the crowd, stirring its emotions, playing on its vanities. He was never terribly good before a large crowd. But he knew how to rule the headlines.

It is well to review what was Senator McCarthy's real achievement. He was a member of the Senate class of 1946 — labeled the Meat Shortage Boys — sent to Congress by an electorate weary of war and rationing. Until his rise to fame in 1950, he had done little to distinguish himself from his classmates. He had not even shown an awareness of the publicity potential of the Red Hunt until after the two-year period during which Alger Hiss was being exposed, tried, retried and finally convicted.

Then, in February 1950, only one month after Hiss received his sentence, McCarthy was off. Brandishing stage-prop documents, which he never let anyone examine, he ingeniously mixed the proper proportions of the misplaced concrete and the farfetched abstraction to meet the requirements of newsmen. As Richard Rovere has pointed out, "SENATOR CHARGES COMMUNIST INFLUENCE IN STATE DEPARTMENT" might have produced a two-inch story on page fifteen of the local newspaper. "OVER TWO HUNDRED WITH COMMUNIST TIES" would have done slightly better. But "205 CARD CARRYING COMMUNISTS" was something else. It was as if the press yearned for the really big lie.

All he had in the way of evidence — and it is not certain he had even this at the very beginning — were charges aired and dropped by a House Committee more than a year previously. But nothing in the procedures of Congress or the press compelled him to reveal what he had. Many of the names he produced had been exposed time and again in the Chicago *Tribune* and the Washington *Times-Herald*. His feat lay in transferring this myth of spy-infested America to more responsible newspapers.

Even the attempts to comply with the dictates of publicity by those appointed to review McCarthy's charges redounded to McCarthy's benefit. Senator Tydings, a politician of the traditional school, scheduled his committee hearings so that each person accused could be given an immediate chance to respond in the vain hope that the denial could catch up with the charge in the battle for the headlines. The only result was to allow McCarthy time to deal out his accusations at greater leisure and to collect still more of his pseudo-evidence, now being funneled to him by all the hate groups in the country. The answers never did catch up with the charges in the headlines.

Responsible newspapers tried hard to live up to the American Society of Newspaper Editors' ethical rule entitled "Fair Play": "A newspaper should not publish unofficial charges affecting reputation or moral character without opportunity given to the accused to be heard." They failed only when the accused, like Owen Lattimore, turned out to be in the wilds of Afghanistan. In practice, it worked as follows: late one afternoon Senator McCarthy might name a person, more likely a series of them. All through the evening the accused's telephone kept ringing. He was told briefly the nature of the charge made against him — let us say, "top Soviet agent" — and asked for a brief reply.

But the dilemma for the reporter and the headline writer remained. McCarthy's charge was controversial and unexpected — a news count of two. The denial was controversial and completely expected — a news count of one. Both were equally lacking in proof. Nobody carries the credentials on his person to prove that he is *not* the "top Soviet agent."

McCarthy held the headlines. Day after day, several times a day in time for the A.M.'s, the P.M.'s, the seven o'clock, and the late evening news, he served up the scabrous material which he was attempting to make the national folklore. He knew the ingredients for the "lead," the "overnight," and the "sidebar." He could evoke the most publicity bounce from the ounce. When his reserves of that commodity he called evidence were running low, he knew how to ration it. He was capable of calling a press conference to announce darkly that he was going to hold an important press conference, thus garnering advance publicity for an event that might or might not come off. Of many things McCarthy was contemptuous, but he never neglected his press relations.

Now, two years after his death, it is fantastic to recall how much McCarthy accomplished. But we should consider first what he did not accomplish. He did not turn up evidence to warrant conviction of any one of the countless number he put the finger on. Even after he became a committee chairman, with the added prerogatives for tracking down and building a case against a suspect, he did not succeed in setting up a single contempt citation that could be sustained in the courts. If the laws were inadequate to deal with the Communist menace, he, as a legislator, never proposed new laws. He was content to "alert" America to the menace.

Even as a demagogue he was notably deficient. He offered no program to channel the frustrations he stirred up. His voting record was remarkably inconsistent — part internationalist, part isolationist, alternately liberal and conservative. Almost his only positive contribution to the legislative agenda was to come out stoutly for 110 per cent farm parity supports.

Yet how great was his impact. Even before he acquired the platform of the committee chairmanship, he had made McCarthyism the focus of our national anxieties. For nearly four years he kept himself and his one-act show in the limelight, competing successfully with a war in Korea and the advent of a new Administration. He managed, with the help of the mass media, to capture the attention of a majority of the American people and to attract the enthusiasms of considerable numbers.

McCarthyism was an unparalleled demonstration of the publicity system gone wild, feeding on the body politic like a cancerous growth. It showed that publicity could be used as a crude instrument with which to bludgeon hapless officials. Not one of the succession of department and agency heads who came up against it was able to find an effective defense against its bludgeoning. Neither of the two Presidents who had to reckon with it ever discovered a satisfactory counterpublicity weapon.

It threw great governmental establishments like the State

Department and the Army into confusion and provoked precipitate decisions on policy and personnel resulting in untold damage. The United States Information Service went through a shake-up from which it has still to recover.

McCarthy's inquiry into espionage at the highly sensitive Fort Monmouth reserve installations was, as Walter Millis described it, "very much like driving a Patton M-47 tank through the heart of an electronic thinking machine on the unfounded suspicion that some of its electronic tubes might have been made in Russia." He bullied a weak and vacillating Secretary of the Army until he succeeded in compromising the integrity of a valiant service.

Finally, he claimed a world audience. Among the free nations, he and his "junketing gumshoes" aroused dark fears about America's capacity to provide wise and dependable leadership in the international community. For the first time he shook the confidence of millions abroad that our devotion to the concepts of liberty and justice were as deep-rooted as they had believed.

All these things he did with the power of publicity. Unlike certain committee chairmen of Congress, he lacked power to insert a crippling rider into legislation or to tamper with an appropriations bill in committee as a way of blackmailing the Executive. He never had the physical means, as his apologists frequently point out, to intimidate or to punish those who aroused his ire. There was no violence, in the ordinary sense of that word, during the reign of McCarthyism. All McCarthy could do was to carry his vendettas into the public headlines. That was enough. It produced unparalleled fear and pusillanimity in Washington.

⁊ ⁊ ⁊

The extent of the communications failure McCarthyism presented can be measured by the fact that few of the reporters who regularly covered McCarthy believed him. Most came to hate and fear him as a cynical liar who was willing to wreak untold havoc to satisfy his own power drive. But though they feared him, it was not intimidation that caused the press to serve as the instrument for McCarthy's rise. Rather it was the inherent vulnerabilities — the frozen patterns of the press — which McCarthy discovered and played upon with unerring skill. "Straight" news, the absolute commandment of most mass media journalism, had become a strait jacket to crush the initiative and the independence of the reporter.

Then, almost as suddenly as it had risen, it was all over. But though there was relief in the passing, it should not be forgotten that McCarthyism was never actually convicted as an extra-legal force in our society violating every Constitutional right and safeguard that stood in its way. The symbolic act of McCarthy's downfall was the vote of censure administered by his Senate colleagues. But they, at the last minute, struck from the resolution all but their disapproval of the way he had abused his fellow Senators. The Vice-President ruled that even the word "censure" no longer remain. For those who witnessed that long dreary climax to McCarthy's career, there was nothing in the Senate's action which gave a sense of the mighty forces of a democracy resolving a weighty Constitutional issue.

McCarthyism was killed as surely as it had been bred by the power of publicity. Nobody, not even the editors, could tell you why. Suddenly, McCarthy was no longer "news." He still struck out at times with his old recklessness. But the reporters left the gallery when he got up to speak. Stories about him kept getting buried inside the paper. The death of the Senator followed two years after the decline of the ism.

The Senator's career needs to be examined for the lessons it provides. McCarthyism showed that the publicity-generating powers of Congress can be a dangerous force when they are not subject to check and review by higher bodies within or without Congress. When Congress abdicates that function, the Executive Branch of government is helpless. Unless there are swift and effective ways of appeal from the assaults of the demagogue, democratic government founders.

McCarthyism demonstrated that public opinion when incessantly nagged by the instantaneous communications of the mass media and prodded by the pollsters is not capable of rendering sure verdicts on matters of great complexity. Rather it is a bastardization of the democratic process to imagine that what captures the public interest because it is repeatedly and distractingly called to its attention must be considered the mandate of the public will.

McCarthyism sought to provide a vocabulary for our fears that had no relevance to the world we actually live in. Responsible men, talking to each other in this synthetic language, for a time lost contact with reality. McCarthyism's greatest threat was not to individual liberty or even to the orderly conduct of government. It corrupted the power to communicate, which is indispensable to men living in a civilized society.

4

The Evolution of the Washington Correspondent

Were it left to me to decide whether we should have a government without newspapers or newspapers without a government, I should not hesitate to prefer the latter. (1787)

It is a melancholy truth that a suppression of the press could not more completely deprive the nation of its benefits, than is done by its abandoned prostitution to falsehood. Nothing can now be believed which is seen in a newspaper. Truth itself becomes suspicious by being put into that polluted vehicle. (1807)

The only security of all is in a free press. (1823)

THOMAS JEFFERSON*

IN A COUNTRY whose founding fathers were so deeply devoted to the institutions of a free press, the early newspapers in America showed remarkably little interest in chronicling the new government. When the Capitol was transferred from Philadelphia to Washington in the late spring of 1800, none of the Philadelphia or New York papers sent along correspondents to cover the story. Indeed, Washington reporting owes its genesis to the suggestion of President-elect Thomas Jefferson to a young journalist, Samuel Harrison Smith, that he move his printing office to the new village on the mudflats of the Potomac. In the fall of 1800, Harrison started a paper, the *National Intelligencer,* published triweekly, which served as a semiofficial organ of the new administration.[1]

* From *The Writings of Thomas Jefferson,* A. A. Lipscomb and A. E. Bergh, ed. (Washington, D. C. 1903–5). Vols. IV, X, and XVIII.

[1] Frank Luther Mott, *American Journalism* (rev. ed., New York, 1950).

The *National Intelligencer* maintained its pre-eminence as an Administration organ and keeper of the congressional journals until Andrew Jackson's Administration, when friends of Old Hickory set up the Washington *Globe,* which in due course received the bulk of the patronage. The *Globe*'s editor, Amos Kendall, was a member of the new President's "Kitchen Cabinet," and played a key role in helping thrash out Jacksonian policies. As one outraged Congressman of that period declared, "He was the President's thinking machine, his writing machine — aye, and his lying machine." Jackson was thoroughly practical in his press relations, it has been recorded, holding very little reverence for the abstract principle of freedom of the press. The *National Intelligencer* once published a list of fifty-seven journalists who had been given federal appointments by the President. The award of government printing contracts as a subsidy for newspaper favorites was not completely abolished until 1860, when the Government Printing Office was established.[2]

During the early years of the republic, out-of-town newspapers relied heavily on news taken, with or without attribution, from these government-subsidized and highly partisan papers. Only gradually the pioneer Washington correspondents began to appear on the scene, usually in the persons of editors come to the nondescript little capital during sessions of Congress to watch government in action. Their communiqués back to their papers were in the form of letters, trenchantly expressing the personal views of the writers. Many of these earliest correspondents made use of pseudonyms. One, Matthew J. Davis, who was biographer and close friend of Aaron Burr, called himself "The Spy in Washington."

Another was described by his paper, the *Evening Post* (New York) as "our airy sprite" and sent his dispatches un-

[2] Mott, *American Journalism.*

der the pseudonym "Ariel." "Ariel," a former Vermont Congressman, was sent to Washington on June 12, 1812, his editor explaining:

> Since the bill declaring war against Great Britain passed the House of Representatives by a very large majority, the public mind, as it was natural to expect, has been uncommonly agitated; and great anxiety has been evinced among men of every political party, to know the fate of this unprecedented measure in the Senate. We waited several days with all the patience we could command, in hopes that our friends in Washington could give us some information on this interesting subject . . .

Evidently, however, "Ariel" proved less than a success, for only one dispatch appeared under his pseudonym, and of this one the editor cautioned, "We do not vouch for the authenticity . . ." A week later, the *Evening Post* carried a local story quoting the "Extract of a way letter (written in extreme haste after the mail was closed) from a gentleman in Washington to another in this city, dated June 16th . . ." Three days *after* the event the readers in New York learned the war bill had passed the Senate by 19 to 13.[3]

The presidential contest of 1824, erupting into a violent struggle which lasted two years and ultimately was thrown into the House of Representatives, made Washington an exciting news center. Soon the more sensitive statesmen were complaining that the intrigues and spying of "hordes" of newspapermen interfered with the performance of their solemn duties. Possibly these "hordes" numbered as many as forty at the peak period compared to the twelve hundred or more journalists in Washington today.

But the Washington press corps was already acquiring privileges and immunities. In 1827, a correspondent for the

[3] Frederick B. Marbut, "Early Washington Correspondents: Some Neglected Pioneers," in the *Journalism Quarterly,* December 1948.

United States Telegraph, having considered himself insulted at a White House reception by the President's son and secretary, John Adams, publicly tweaked the young man's nose when they later met in a Capitol corridor. Despite an angry presidential demand for a congressional investigation the correspondent, backed by his press colleagues, reportedly suffered no disciplining.[4]

It is a matter of dispute who holds the honor of being the first regular Washington correspondent. A principal contender was Nathaniel Carter, senior editor of the New York *Statesman and Evening Advertiser,* who came to Washington in late 1822 to provide an account of the proceedings of Congress and, in his words, "the latest intelligence of every description which can be obtained at the seat of government." During his second winter in Washington, Carter announced in his dispatch that he was altering his byline. "At the suggestion of a valuable friend . . . I have concluded . . . to amend the caption of my correspondence by striking out the word 'editorial' and inserting the word 'Washington.' Our readers will readily perceive that this amendment will give me more latitude and open a wider field for variety . . ." It was the first use of the phrase "Washington Correspondence" applied to a regular newspaper feature.[5]

Mr. Carter was a voluminous correspondent. One of his dispatches airs a still familiar grievance: "Nearly the whole of this day has been occupied with Mr. Webster's speech in favor of the Greeks . . . Our readers of course expect a sketch and at six o'clock in the evening, after undergoing the fatigue of writing three hours and taking notes without rising from my seat, I sit down for the purpose of reporting before the mail closes, one of the most argumentative and

[4] Duncan Aikman, "Prehistory," in *Dateline: Washington,* Cabell Phillips and Others, eds. (Garden City, N. Y., 1949).

[5] Marbut, "Early Washington Correspondents."

elaborate speeches, probably ever delivered in the House of Representatives . . ." His account of the debate ran three full columns and was followed on succeeding days by eight more columns devoted to the same subject.[6]

Another correspondent during this period dispatched to his paper an early prototype of today's "background" story:

> Rumors of an unpleasant nature are afloat this morning, but I cannot in time for the post ascertain if there be any foundation for them. It is said that a challenge has passed between an official functionary of the highest rank and another who is little his inferior in official rank, and that it has been accepted. The misunderstanding is said to have risen out of recent circumstances just *bruited* to the world. The rumor further states that this affair will expedite the dissolution of the present cabinet. I know not what degree of credence is due to the report.[7]

His not-for-attribution reportage compares favorably in modesty, if not intelligibility, with more recent examples of this frustrating brand of journalism.

Another pioneer of the Washington press corps was James Gordon Bennett, who afterward won greater fame as founder and editor of the New York *Herald*. Bennett, having come across a book of Walpole's letters in the Library of Congress, adopted their style in his own reports. He told what went on at the social gatherings, and generally gave a lively account of the behind-the-scenes activities in the nation's capital. Since Bennett's time, according to one press historian, "Gossip and chat have been recognized features of Washington correspondence." [8]

These and a half-dozen others were the progenitors. They put up at the hotels and boarding houses where room and board could be had for a maximum of $35 a month, free

[6] New York *Advertiser,* January 24, 28, 31, February 2, 1824.

[7] "From Our Correspondent, Washington, Jan. 8, 1830," in the Charleston *Courier,* January 14, 1830.

[8] Marbut, "Early Washington Correspondents."

whiskey included; they wrote three or four dispatches a week for fees ranging between three dollars and five dollars apiece; and somehow they managed to make out. By the end of Jackson's Administration in 1837, the letter writer from Washington was definitely on the way to becoming a recognizable spot-news correspondent.[9]

By 1841, James Gordon Bennett, now running the New York *Herald,* had set up at the reputed cost of two hundred dollars a week the first Washington bureau with regular courier service to New York. The New York *Sun* and the *Tribune* of Mr. Horace Greeley soon followed his example. But the reporting of Washington was still only a seasonal occupation. Right up to the Civil War, all the out-of-town correspondents fled the capital upon the adjournment of Congress each summer.

✓ ✓ ✓

The pre-Civil War period was predominantly an era of personal journalism, no longer dictated by purely partisan interests, but not yet refined by concepts of objectivity toward those individuals and issues the reporter and his editor might like or dislike. During the numerous congressional battles leading up to the Civil War, the reporting from Washington did little to inject a dispassionate note into the drama. A report from the correspondent "Index" in the March 23, 1858, New York *Tribune,* gave the following account of a Senate speech by Senator Robert Toombs, of Georgia, during the fight over admission of Kansas into the Union:

> It is a sad instance of the wretched effect which the Africanization of the South has had upon even her strongest minds, that a man like Mr. Toombs should feel himself compelled to rise as he did today, in the face of the Amer-

[9] Aikman, "Prehistory," in *Dateline: Washington.*

> ican Senate and the American people, and debase himself by prostituting his powers of speech and argument to the vain task of proving that to be true which he knows to be false, and that to be sound which he knows to be rotten . . .

The reporter's description of one Senator might be, "small in stature; dresses carefully and neatly; has a soft catlike step; a fawning, sinister smile; a keen, snaky eye; a look and address now bold and audacious, and then cringing and deprecatory; his whole air and mien suggesting a subdued combination of Judas Iscariot with Uriah Heep." His speech, of course, was "false to truth, to humanity and to decency . . ." On the other hand, the speech of the Senator admired by the reporter was "full of marrow and grit, and enunciated with a courage which did one's heart good to hear. No mealy-mouthed phrases . . . but strong and stirring old English, that had the ring of the true metal." [10]

The first telegraphic news dispatch to clatter out of Washington appeared in the Baltimore *Patriot* on May 25, 1844, and set the pattern for the terse to the point of unintelligible reporting of the wire services. It read *in toto:* "One o'clock —There has just been made a motion in the House to go into Committee of the Whole on the Oregon question. Rejected—Ayes, 79; Nays, 86." Of course, a mitigating factor for such brevity was the exorbitant cost of one cent per character transmitted.[11] But before long, all the New York news-

[10] Bernard A. Weisberger, *Reporters for the Union* (Boston, 1953).

[11] Henry David Thoreau, who the very next year retired to the woods, had a biting comment to make in *Walden* about this new development: "We are in great haste to construct a magnetic telegraph from Maine to Texas: but Maine and Texas, it may be, have nothing important to communicate. Either is in such a predicament as the man who is anxious to be introduced to a distinguished deaf woman, but when he is presented, and one end of her ear trumpet is put into his hand, has nothing to say . . . We are eager to tunnel under the Atlantic and bring the old world some weeks nearer to the new; but perchance the first news which will leak through into the broad, flapping American ear will be that the Princess Adelaide has the whooping cough."

papers were carrying their special column of Washington news, headed "By Magnetic Telegraph."

The approach of the Civil War firmly institutionalized the role of the Washington correspondent. For the first time a reporter was assigned full time to cover the President-elect. This ancestor of the modern White House correspondent, a twenty-five-year-old Middle Westerner, Henry Villard, of the Associated Press, though tremendously excited by his novel and important mission, failed to take notes on Mr. Lincoln's farewell speech before the departure for Washington. On the train, Lincoln obligingly wrote it out for him in pencil and Villard was able to file his dispatch at the first telegraph station.[12]

It was during this period that the young Henry Adams, who had come to Washington to serve as secretary to his Congressman father, embarked secretly on the role of Washington correspondent for the Boston *Advertiser,* a Republican paper whose editor, Charles Hale, was his good friend. Though his columns were anonymous, the young Adams knew much the same heady sensation of power and participation that excites the columnist in Washington today. "Drawn into the vortex of behind-the-scenes negotiation, Henry experienced a sense of 'continual intoxication,' " a biographer has noted. Adams himself wrote somewhat immodestly in a letter to his brother that it was "magnificent to feel strong and quiet in all this row, and see one's own path clear through all the chaos." [13]

Like a nineteenth-century Joseph Alsop, Adams advised his brother that his reports to the *Advertiser* would be on "the crescendo principle" and urged that "if the battle 'should wax hot,' and Charles Hale does not rise to it, you must thumbscrew him a little." He was unabashed at the

[12] Oliver Gramling, *AP: The Story of News* (New York, 1940).
[13] Ernest Samuels, *The Young Henry Adams* (Cambridge, 1948).

idea of using his column as an instrument of influence and special pleading rather than as a vehicle for enlightening his readers. When his father and Charles Sumner came close to a disastrous rupture, Adams wrote columns deliberately designed to flatter and mollify Sumner.

⸙ ⸙ ⸙

The approaching war more than doubled the correspondents in Washington. A body of "guerilla news raiders" invaded the capital, many of them little interested in the higher pursuits of journalism. There were other profitable occupations beside the business of writing news. One dyspeptic commentator of the time claimed that the newspapers kept agents in Washington ready to negotiate with applicants for contracts, solicitors of private bills, lobbyists, or others who might "stand in need of newspaper assistance."[14]

A correspondent of the early war period, on leaving Washington, wrote a bitter farewell which would evoke sympathetic agreement among a good many overworked bureau chiefs today. He spoke of his gratitude at being relieved of

> the business of general agent in the city of Washington for all people who happen to take the *New York Tribune* or who know me in person or by name . . . For nine months I have borne its burden, being afflicted during that long time with the applications for about everything that the heart of man can desire out of a national capital . . . from requests for authority to raise brigades down to the procurement of discharges from the ranks of boys, runaways from their mothers' homes . . . to orders for garden seeds from the Patent Office, and memorial bowie knives from . . . Bull Run . . .[15]

[14] Lambert A. Wilmer, *Our Press Gang* (Philadelphia, 1859).
[15] Weisberger, *Reporters for the Union.*

The wartime capital provided a rich news field for the more enterprising reporters. Some by their prodding helped to bring about the ouster of Lincoln's first Secretary of War, Simon Cameron, for alleged graft — by no means the last high-ranking official to be brought down by the newsmen.

After the disastrous battle of Bull Run, censorship was clapped down on Washington and with censorship came the problems of a government policy for dealing with members of the press. The first impromptu arrangement was for the representative of the Associated Press to serve as liaison between the War Cabinet and the newspapermen in handing out news items. Only one snag developed. Representatives of local newspapers in Washington were made to wait for the news to be telegraphed to New York and back again before it was given to them. At the intervention of President Lincoln the practice was altered.[16]

Censorship during the Civil War period was by all accounts a grim and unsuccessful effort. Correspondents found themselves subjected to all manner of arbitrary harassment. Evidently the government was as sinned against as sinning, for the news that reporters did get past the censor into their papers was quite considerable. Jefferson Davis and other leaders of the Confederacy made diligent efforts to obtain Northern papers for news of troop movements and vessel destinations.[17]

Censorship had its curious consequences. One rule promulgated by the War Department as a way to fix responsibility required all war stories to bear the byline of the correspondent. This helped to create the first big name reporters whose fame was independent of their papers. Their need for copy also brought the beginning of modern press agentry. As one historian has written, "Making heroes was in some respects a natural preoccupation for the correspondents. The country

[16] James Melvin Lee, *History of American Journalism* (Boston, 1917).
[17] Mott, *American Journalism.*

fidgeted over the morning papers impatiently, looking for the one man with the ready answer or shortcut which would bring a quick return out of the growing national investment in manpower, energy and cash . . . The reporters who became barkers for these 'geniuses' were no more gullible than most, but their positions made their errors more damaging." [18]

There were more cynical explanations. The Chicago *Tribune,* ever a snide commentator on its fellow journalists, declared in 1862, "Much of the laudatory writing of the war was emitted by 'army correspondents, with bellies full from the mess tables of Major Generals . . .' "

Not all of the generals were susceptible to this new art. General William Tecumseh Sherman regularly banished correspondents from his theater of operation, and once remarked when he learned that three of them had been killed, "Good! Now we shall have news from hell before breakfast." But the dapper General McClellan, cultivated and colorful, was well suited to the needs of his press agents. The newspapers, particularly the New York *Herald,* made of McClellan an almost legendary figure of military prowess before President Lincoln was finally obliged to relieve him because of his inept command.

By the end of the war the press corps in Washington was booming and had already formed the first of the numerous fraternal organizations for promoting good fellowship and exacting respect from the politicians. Beginning to develop within the press, too, were more modern notions about reporting. The heads of the Associated Press were troubled by the warped opinions and the twisted reports in news columns, which had helped stir sectional antipathies before the war. They started to lay down rules about "straight" reporting which would avoid all bias and alienate none of their numerous member papers.

By 1867, there were forty-nine correspondents listed in the

[18] Weisberger, *Reporters for the Union.*

congressional Press Galleries, including twenty-six telegraphic reporters. A number of reporters were prominent celebrities in their own right and the salaries of at least two or three were said to exceed $12,000 a year. The press corps, for the most part, was housed in comfortable old rookeries on lower Fourteenth Street, which came to be known as Newspaper Row.

The press interview, an American innovation as a formal technique, came into its own. Andrew Johnson was the first President to be formally "interviewed" for a newspaper story. A correspondent could gain fame and riches by being granted special privileges in this not too subtle form of press agentry. R. deB. Keim of the New York *Herald* bureau is said to have made a comfortable fortune selling his many interviews with General Ulysses Grant, to whom he had ready access. The practice soon got out of bounds. An article in the *Nation* at the time remarked that " 'the interview' as presently managed is generally the joint project of some humbug of a hack politician and another humbug of a reporter."

While technology was revolutionizing the press in general with the inventions of the linotype, the rotary press, and the automatic newspaper folding machines, the Washington correspondent was bolstered by the arrival of two instruments of modern pressdom: the typewriter and the telephone. The latter, in particular, served to broaden his horizons, though not unfortunately to reduce his labors. In the evenings the new telephone at the White House was reportedly answered by Grover Cleveland in person. Press corps folklore has it that once a brash young correspondent won a five-dollar bet by ringing up the President and asking him if there was any news.

By the turn of the century, the newspapers of the nation were fed a steady flow of telegraphic news from Washington. The men of the press held lofty notions about their contributions to statecraft. The Associated Press, for example, claims practically singlehanded credit for its General Manager, Melville E. Stone, in negotiating the Peace Treaty of Portsmouth, which ended the 1905 Russo-Japanese War. According to the history of this association, Stone called on President Theodore Roosevelt, "outlined the terms on which he thought peace could be reached and suggested that the President cable the German Kaiser to use his influence with the Czar to have them accepted." The AP then reported to its readers the drama it had helped to stage.[19]

Concepts of news had begun to have an impact in the highest realms of government policy making. In 1904 a wealthy American, Ion Perdicaris, was seized and held for ransom by a Mediterranean bandit chieftain named Raisuli. Secretary of State John Hay was engaged in making diplomatic representations to the Sultan of Morocco to obtain the American's release. The Associated Press history gives an inside account of this episode:

> [Hay] was completing a draft of his note when Edwin M. Hood dropped in on his customary State Department round. Hood, of the [AP's] Washington staff, had been reporting the activities of the government for years. He had entree everywhere, was the confidant of many high officials . . . Hay and Hood were old friends and the Secretary welcomed an outside opinion on the message.
>
> Hood scanned the document. The message was long, formal, and full of the phraseology dictated by protocol and diplomatic usage. Hood shook his head.
>
> "Well?" asked Hay.
>
> "I'm afraid you're slipping, Mr. Secretary," the correspondent smiled. "If I were you, I'd boil all this down to five words."
>
> He produced a pencil and scribbled five words which re-

[19] Gramling, *AP: The Story of News.*

duced Hay's long note to the simplest terms. He handed his suggestion to the secretary:

"Perdicaris alive or Raisuli dead."

Whatever its effect on Mr. Perdicaris' release, this headline version of diplomacy captured the public imagination and was used to good effect by Roosevelt during his political campaigning that year. Ironically, the phrase years later became a favorite quotation of Senator Joseph McCarthy when he was attacking Secretary of State Acheson for his less flamboyant diplomatic methods.

✓ ✓ ✓

The twentieth-century history of the Washington press corps is one of growth and flowering. By 1908 correspondents had arrived in such numbers that they joined to form the National Press Club. One oldtimer has explained their motivation: "They had to keep in contact with one another professionally. For them news was a perpetually threatening river to be watched around the clock. And the watchers must watch the watchers to survive. They must mingle." [20]

And mingle they do at the Press Club headquarters, which has come to be the central professional and social institution of the press corps. Within two decades, the National Press Club arranged the construction of the massive building in the heart of Washington where many of the correspondents have their offices. The Club's auditorium on the thirteenth floor is an automatic stop-off point on the itinerary of almost every head of state, crowned sovereign, or other potentate who makes his way to Washington. At gatherings it is traditional for the club president to subject the great and near-great of Washington to outrageous spoofing. No one would dare to protest these liberties in the press's own sanctum.

[20] Scott Hart, "From Such a Bond," in *Dateline: Washington.*

The National Press Club has its less glamorous side. A good deal of the news that emanates from there is gained by bending the elbow rather than wearing out shoe leather. The Club's bar is the fulcrum for the exertions of every pressure group that seeks to work its will within the nation's capital. Much of the time the lobbyists, the public relations men, and the various hangers-on outnumber the working reporters in attendance.

Other groups contribute to the reporter's busy organization life. They include the Overseas Writers Club, which specializes in background luncheons mostly on foreign policy matters, the White House Correspondents Association, the Washington Chapter of Sigma Delta Chi, honorary press fraternity, and, most eminent of all, the Gridiron Club. The last, described as the Skull and Bones of the Washington campus, dates back to 1885, limits its membership to fifty, and maintains considerable social prestige because of its semiannual dinners. Politicians vie for invitations to the festivities at which they are panned mercilessly in the farcical satires staged by the reporters.

In 1912, when Bascom Timmons, probably the oldest member of the press corps today, arrived in Washington, two leading correspondents predicted to him that Woodrow Wilson's victory would bring a halt to centralization of government and that Washington would certainly recede as a news center. But government grew and so did the numbers of reporters. Their expansion over the half century was to be almost ten fold.

One by one there appeared on the Washington scene the various appurtenances necessary for dealing with a press that had become a big business in the capital. The press conference, enabling politicians and officials to handle reporters in the mass, gradually broadened from an exclusive presidential prerogative to become a device for every Cabinet officer, agency head, member of Congress or aspiring politician.

Its evolution has been enormously haphazard, and its usefulness has ranged widely according to the precepts of those employing it. Still, a thoughtful observer like Erwin Canham has hailed the press conference as "the fifth wheel of Democracy," claiming that it introduced the interpellative devices of English and French parliamentary government into the less flexible pattern of American politics.[21]

In 1910, Congress, while probing into the Bureau of the Census, heard its director admit that "for about six months now, we have had a person whose principal duty is to act as what might properly be called, I suppose, a press agent." This first of the government publicity men, a former newspaperman named Whitman Osgood, was carried on the books for $8 a day under the title "expert special agent." His successors, listed as press secretaries, information officers, and special assistants, were to become familiar figures to the reporter in Washington. And Congress, though always suspicious of the Executive department's attempts to feed news to the press, was soon employing these selfsame experts for its own uses.

With the information men came their formal product — the "handout" or official news release published by the government office for the use of the press. Analysis of a typical week's output has revealed nearly three hundred such handouts containing over two hundred thousand words, more voluminous, if a great deal less readable, than a good-sized novel. They have become the subject of ever recurring debates between government and the editors. The latter fear them as an insidious evil intended to beguile their reporters and prevent independent investigations. But they continue to flourish, filling the long table at the National Press Club and being slipped with clocklike regularity through the reporter's letter slot. In simple truth, they are the most efficient way to transmit the vast bulk of the routine news about govern-

[21] See Chapter 8.

ment. For the reporter the beguiling fact is that government itself has become so big and so complex that he has not enough time to do the investigating he considers necessary.

One more innovation of big-time Washington reporting: the correspondent began the exchange of "black sheets," which simply meant he engaged in cooperative plagiarism with fellow reporters by exchanging carbon copies of stories. The practice flourished and still flourishes fairly freely in the steamy news-barren months of late summer after Congress has gone home. In less obvious form it can be traced through the endless reiteration of a story by less enterprising reporters once it has "broken" in the *Times,* the *Herald Tribune,* or some with a hardworking Washington bureau.

In 1921, Walter Lippmann declared that "within the life of the generation now in control of affairs, persuasion has become a self-conscious art and a regular organ of popular government." [22] An instance he possibly had in mind was the Senate fight over ratification of the League of Nations when the "little band of willful men" displayed remarkable skill in manipulating the channels of communication for their own ends. As one reporter, who covered that fight, has written, "Senator George H. Moses of New Hampshire plotted the strategy of stealing headlines. There was a continuous flow of material to the black-sheeters. Moses regimented the League opponents' statements and often ghosted them. Let Senator Gilbert M. Hitchcock of Nebraska, leader of the ratificationists, make a day-long exposition for his cause, and Moses was ready with a statement of strategy fathered by Jim Reed, Borah, Johnson, or Brandegee. It would be sufficiently hot to take the headlines away from Hitchcock from coast to coast." [23]

Members of the press were by no means innocent bystand-

[22] Walter Lippmann, *Public Opinion* (New York, 1922).

[23] Bascom N. Timmons, "This Is How It Used to Be," in *Dateline: Washington.*

ers. The columnist Ray Tucker has described the way a sma
group of correspondents

> . . . conspired hourly with the "irreconcilables" and per
> formed service far beyond the call of newspaper duty. They
> tipped off most of the Congressmen to Wilsonian statements
> and maneuvers, and started Senatorial counterattacks before
> the War president could unlimber his orators. They wrote
> phillipics for the Borahs, Johnsons; and Reeds, cooked up
> interviews . . . carried on independent res[illegible]rch into t[illegible]
> League's implications, dug up secret materi[illegible] dis-
> patches bristled with personal hostility to the League, and
> the carbon copies which they distributed to pro-Wilson
> writers affected even the latter's supposedly favorable ar-
> ticles. The Covenant was defeated by the Senate press gallery
> long before it was finally rejected by the Senate.[24]

Radio joined the mass media. In 1923, President Warren G. Harding received the first fan telegram ever sent to a President after a radio speech. "We heard you as plainly as if you had been in our living room," wired Senator William M. Calder, reportedly pleasing the President immensely. In those days, as the Columbia Broadcasting System's Washington executive Theodore Koop has remarked wistfully, nobody cared about the content of radio so long as the voice was intelligible.

By a decade later, CBS had inaugurated its own news service to compete with the press associations. Its opening feature was an exclusive interview with Senator William E. Borah of Idaho on the burning question of recognizing Soviet Russia. CBS was jubilant next day when the *New York Times* reprinted Borah's views on page one. To this day, the networks are apt to measure the success of their news shows by the space accorded them in the *Times*.

Radio reporting was off to a self-conscious start. Not many

[24] Ray Tucker, "Part-Time Statesmen," in *Collier's*, October 28, 1933.

years later, network reporters in Washington were to number nearly two hundred, claiming special galleries of their own in the House and Senate.

Despite all the changes, reporting in Washington before the Great Depression and the New Deal had not changed too much in its fundamentals. The Washington correspondent was still a fairly limited political animal. He thought, as one reporter has put it, that "government pump priming referred to a late afternoon slug of the real stuff in House Speaker Nicholas Longworth's office." [25] The White House was a dull news source. At an afternoon press conference President Calvin Coolidge might flip through fifty or more of the written questions that had to be submitted in advance and finally concentrate on the subject of the chrysanthemum show being held in the city. Other news sources in the Executive departments were largely undeveloped, although Herbert Hoover did his best to make Commerce a lively place for the reporter. But on the Hill, the reporter found plenty to occupy him. He teamed up with the Senator to launch the investigations which knocked the underpinnings out from under the administrations of that unhappy decade. It was, for example, reporter Paul Y. Anderson who helped feed Senator Walsh the questions that exploded the great Teapot Dome scandals.

By the arrival of the 1930's, the Washington correspondent was certainly an important functionary about town. He had achieved status, prestige, and continuing power in the still fairly loose operation of government. He, like the official, was comparatively unsophisticated. He had few specialties. His understanding was still quite limited. He, even as government itself, was unprepared for — largely unaware of — the vast changes that lay just ahead.

[25] Fletcher Knebel, "The Placid Twenties," in *Dateline: Washington.*

5

Washington Reporting Tries to Come of Age

> We never covered Washington in the '20's. We covered the Senate. You wasted your time downtown.
>
> RAYMOND P. BRANDT*

THE GREAT DEPRESSION and the accompanying New Deal ushered in a new era of Washington journalism. It created news in quantity and complexity that threatened for a time to overwhelm the poor correspondent. The first Hundred Days of the Roosevelt Administration caused him severe growing pains. Such strange new subjects as banking and monetary policy, labor relations, and the rest suddenly had to be added to his vocabulary and, hopefully, his understanding.

The New Deal years produced qualitative as well as quantitative change in Washington reporting. News production became a bigger business than ever, geared to year-round output. Gone were the days when the reporter left Washington with the adjournment of Congress. Reporting grew compartmentalized, the reporter became something of a specialist, often as expert as the official on matters of agriculture, utility

* Quoted by Fletcher Knebel in "The Placid Twenties," *Dateline: Washington,* Cabell Phillips and Others, eds. (Garden City, N. Y., 1949).

regulation, civil aeronautics, and the rest. Even on Capitol Hill there was a new division of labor among the press representatives. There had to be. News was too fast breaking, too diverse, too complicated to permit the former loose arrangements. The press forsook its old carefree ways just as government did.

The old-fashioned general-assignment reporter in Washington, who nibbled at news wherever he could find it, survived but in reduced circumstances. A number of big city dailies across the country have continued to keep one- and two-man bureaus whose reporters are permitted to range widely between local-interest stories and national affairs. Some turn out highly creditable work. But in a period of enormous expansion in personnel and expenditure, this form of coverage has not held its own. In its place, Washington reporting has discovered new methods of organization, new ways of packaging news in response to the newly felt needs and the newly developed media of communication.

As a group, the reporters have made Washington the most thoroughly covered and most heavily reported capital in the world. Well over one hundred thousand words daily pour out on wire, radio, and video waves. In periods of peak stress, the sheer productive capacity of this great industry belies the imagination. The two-hundred-dollar weekly budget of the old New York *Herald* bureau has been displaced by budgets ranging into the tens of thousands of dollars in the present-day network, wire service, and newsweekly bureaus.

Journalism moved to keep up with the changing times. Yet it would be preposterous to argue that reporting has met the enormous challenge confronting it. For the dimension of the challenge goes beyond the requirements of speed, specialization, and clever new ways of packaging. It is, rather, to be measured by how well the citizens of a democracy, whose system of government is dependent on informed public opinion, can get the essential facts to permit them to form reasoned judgments. Viewed in these terms, reporting from Washington provides cause for sober and troubled consideration.

❦ ❦ ❦

Fastest to flower among the new genres of reporting was the syndicated Washington columnist. Even before the 1930's there had been pioneers. Among the first of them was David Lawrence, who a decade earlier began to include in the shirttail of his daily story for the New York *Evening Post* a succinct interpretation of the "why" of things happening in the nation's capital. Always an extraordinarily successful businessman, Lawrence, who still writes a column and edits *U.S. News & World Report,* was able to peddle his efforts to other papers.

A second entrepreneur in this field was Paul Mallon, a United Press reporter on the Hill, who in 1929 set out to nullify the Senate practice of taking certain votes in secret session. He did it by the simple method of tabulating the roll call on each vote with the help of a few obliging Senators and publishing his results. Mallon destroyed the Senate secrecy and won for himself a certain amount of national fame. His subsequent five-days-a-week feature, "News Behind the News," is considered the progenitor of "the revelatory, gossipy, fact-plus-hunch-plus-opinion column." [1]

But it took the Depression, with its uncertainties, its disillusionment, and its cynicism toward conventional news sources to bring the Golden Age of the columnists. Close to two hundred sprang into existence between 1930 and 1934. Many disappeared as rapidly as they came, but others sur-

[1] Cabell Phillips, "Autocrats of the Breakfast Table," in *Dateline: Washington.*

vived and flourished. Approximately fifty syndicated columnists, it is estimated, earn a regular livelihood in Washington. Far fewer, however, have any degree of national prominence.

The syndicated column has been peculiar to America. In no other country is the packaged output of a single journalist, frequently highly opinionated, distributed to millions of readers via newspapers which may hold diametrically opposite editorial views. It has made the Washington columnist a formidable figure. He consorts with the mighty and keeps Cabinet members in fear and trembling. His arrogance is legendary. One of them could slam his fist down on the desk of a very highly placed government official and declare angrily, "Sir, you have just wasted a half hour of my time." Like the young Henry Adams, he never doubts that he sees his path "clear through all the chaos." Government programs have been altered to win his approval or avoid his wrath.

Yet, there are vulnerabilities to this calling. In discarding one master he becomes the servant of many. The late Tom Stokes, a veteran columnist for Scripps-Howard, vividly described his drawbacks:

> He is sold as a package thrown in with a comic strip and a sports feature. He is reviled by the editor and used as a whipping boy or, alternatively, as a lightning rod to deflect criticism from the newspaper's own editorials. He is bought in a lump by the big papers and run at the editor's whim. He is demanded by the smaller papers on a five-day-a-week basis because "that space has got to be filled and we can't spare anybody to fill it." For the still smaller papers, even though he is sold dirt cheap, he is not economically feasible and so he is displaced by the canned features and editorials given out gratis by NAM and other special interest groups.[2]

[2] Personal interview, July 1956.

The gripes are not all on the columnist's side. Sevellon Brown, editor of the Providence *Journal,* has voiced qualms felt by the more serious editors, "Our chief quarrel with the national syndicated news columnists is that most of them — because they practice in a fiercely competitive field and are striving for fabulous incomes from fabulous circulations — are too concerned with posturing for attention value, appeal far more to the emotions than to the mind, and offer less common sense than verbal fireworks."

It is a demanding occupation — to encapsulate the universe on a multiweekly basis. A British observer of the American scene has prescribed the philosophical requirements for this journalistic entrepreneur who doesn't exist in England: [3] "[The columnist] must . . . have a well-stored mind and the integrated outlook of a man who has worked out his basic assumptions to the point where they give him a reasoned *Weltanschauung*. These attributes are necessarily rare. Yet without them a columnist is merely a performer, someone with technique and after that nothing. His stock in trade consists of his skill in linking new topics to old prejudices. Few American columnists have any better equipment."

Few, indeed, have lived up to these high criteria. Walter Lippmann, the most enduring of the Washington columnists, has probably come the closest. He has never pretended to deal in behind-the-scenes sensation. For nearly three decades he has examined the confused fragments of daily events with a clear, perceptive intellect. At times his column has stood as a solitary counterpoise to the massive policy-forming apparatus of the State Department. It provides a moderate, yet incisive, viewpoint on the nation's most muddled domestic issues such as race relations. Lippmann has been read and quoted by foreign heads of government, including Premier Khrushchev of the Soviet Union. No other country has quite his counterpart in journalism.

[3] Charles Curran, "AOT in U.S.A.," in *Encounter,* May 1958.

Joseph Alsop, also serious and successful as a columnist, can claim to have a reasoned *Weltanschauung*. Shortly after the Second World War Alsop flatly predicted to the Signet Society of Harvard that the cause of Western man was lost. In an eloquent comparison of our fate to that of the Spartans at the battle of Thermopylae, he urged free men today, like the ancient Greeks, to "comb their golden hair in the sunlight and prepare to die bravely."

Such a philosophy has provided Alsop enormous clarity of purpose. As Dr. Samuel Johnson once remarked, "Depend on it, when a man knows he is going to be hanged in a fortnight, it concentrates his mind wonderfully." No one has been more courageous than Alsop in resisting false prophets like McCarthy who would pervert Western civilization while pretending to save it. At the same time, no columnist has been more relentless in criticizing public leaders not prepared to make the hero's effort against the Soviets. Alsop's admonitions sometimes range from the shrill to the near hysteric. At his best, he is a superb and untiring reporter. His uncanny ability to delve into the most classified areas of military strategy has enraged the President and broken up National Security Council meetings.

The *Weltanschauung* of Drew Pearson consists mostly of pious platitudes about "making democracy live" and sophomoric suggestions that the label SOB, regularly pinned on him by politicians, stands for "Servant of Brotherhood." His column "Washington Merry-Go-Round" is important because it is the most prominent of the hurdy-gurdy brand of journalism that disturbs serious journalists and readers alike. His phenomenal inaccuracy with names, dates, places, and the other elemental details of reporting casts suspicion on everything he writes.

Pearson's columns contain bad writing and phony dramatics. He never hesitates to re-create secret conversations and pass them off as direct quotations. On occasion, while promoting pet politicians or hounding others, he has been guilty of shockingly bad judgment. His bitter personal attack on Secretary Forrestal, his report of an Eisenhower seizure that never occurred, and his intimate but unsustained description of a plot by Nixon to take over the reins of power — these and other episodes show gross irresponsibility.

Equally serious, Pearson undermines the field of investigative reporting for other journalists who cannot match him for pure shock value. One reporter has noted, "In the American government the leak is functional and Pearson has channelized it." Yet he never warns his readers that much of the inside dope comes from highly prejudiced sources and, though deserving attention, should be examined skeptically.

Yet, it is not possible to dismiss Pearson lightly. In a city where powerful vested interests seek privilege, he has fought them unsparingly. He does not reverence the traditional sacred cows. Not even the Federal Bureau of Investigation is immune to his criticism. Unlike most publicists, he has not allowed mass circulation to exact from him a diluted product.

Pearson, driven by a Quaker sense of rectitude, is habitually for the underdog. Amid the complex tangle of Washington issues, he has been uncommonly shrewd in discerning between the good and the evil. He counts to his credit the jailing of four Congressmen exposed in his columns. Countless others pursue righteousness from fear of being similarly pointed out.

It is too early to predict the future of the Washington columnist. The ranks are still largely filled with the first generation, and none of the recent newcomers has had the impact of some of the oldtimers. A successor to Walter Lippmann, if there is to be one, has yet to show himself. Partly this failure of regeneration may be due to the publishers who, more business-minded than in former days, desire a less

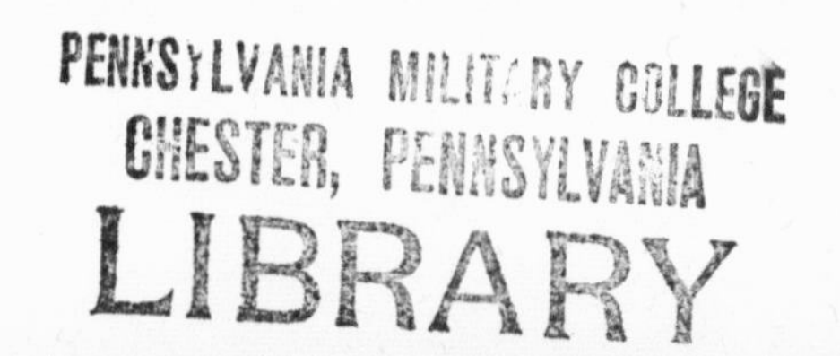

controversial breed. Partly it is due to the fact that the era in which we live, vastly different from the New Deal era, presents problems so complex and diverse that even the omniscient columnist is baffled. Working usually without research assistance, he finds himself enormously strained in trying to come up with fresh intelligence and new perspectives several times weekly.

✓ ✓ ✓

The news weekly brought still another reporter to Washington, generally youthful, college-trained, well paid, and equipped with a somewhat different set of instincts from those of his colleagues on the dailies. He became adept at ferreting out the obscure little facts that would give narrative excitement to a story: "James Campbell Hagerty left his pale green office, walked 30 brisk steps down the hall, opened a door and took seven more paces to the desk of the President of the U.S."[4]

He was member of a publication that in the words of Time, Inc. was to be "written as if by one man for one man." The founders of *Time,* Henry Luce and Briton Hadden, had concluded that "People are uninformed because no publication has adapted itself to the time which busy men are able to spend on simply keeping informed." With the news more tightly organized and crisply laid out, with a whole new vocabulary and syntax for making it lively and readable, *Time* climbed steadily toward a multimillion circulation, followed at a respectable rate by its competitors. The news magazine became a powerful instrument for shaping public opinion.

The news-weekly reporter was supposed to be "fair" not "impartial."[5] "The responsible journalist," announced

[4] *Time,* January 27, 1958.
[5] *Time,* March 8, 1948.

Time's editors, "is 'partial' to that interpretation of the facts which seems to him to fit things as they are. He is fair in not twisting the facts to support his view, in not suppressing the facts that support a different view."

Because of wealth and organization, the news magazine has been able to devote enormous research facilities to the preparation of a story. Geared to the weekly rather than the daily production schedule it avoids many of the frenetic deadline crises that afflict the newspaper and produce inevitable distortions. Ideally, the news magazines could offer unlimited scope for first-rate reporting which is carried to a national audience. They could provide an acceptable and in many ways preferable substitute for the great national dailies which are prevalent in Great Britain and even the Soviet Union but have never been possible in America.

Yet, the news weeklies have so far fallen short of any such potential. Critics dispute their brand of journalism in strong terms. In the words of one, " . . . *Time* satisfies its readers' craving for reality by creating a pseudo-reality, the pretended inside knowledge . . . which is really a kind of processing of facts garnered by researchers and interwoven with the opinions of *Time* editors. And, aside from the slanting given a story on principle, the *Time* method itself, with its division of labor and anonymity, makes accuracy difficult." [6]

There is need, of course, for journals of opinion. But the news magazine seeks to disguise its opinions with a synthetic news treatment. Its editors have no hard and fast rules about what can and cannot be done to the reporter's copy. They show no restraint in reshaping the reality that flows across their desks in dispatch form to suit certain preconceived and sometimes highly partisan notions. Too often in reading the news magazine account of an event he has personally ob-

[6] Mary McCarthy, "The Menace to Free Journalism in America," in *The Listener*, May 14, 1953.

served, the reporter is aware of facts "twisted" or facts "left out." The bias of *Time* is painfully obvious at times. George E. Allen, who was a "crony" and a "clown" when he associated with Truman, became a "Washington lawyer" and "friend of Presidents" when he transferred his company to Eisenhower.

As one analyst has concluded:

> It is typical of *Time*'s political reporting that the political world is generally divided into the forces of evil and the forces of virtue . . . In *Time* villains "cry"; the heroes "solemnly state" . . . The outstanding character of the political reporting . . . is that without telling the reader why, the magazine surrounds personalities with an emotional aura, sometimes with adjectives, sometimes with verbs, sometimes with figures of speech. Stylistically, the result is the most dramatic, crisp and evocative language in the news profession. But politically it is a vapor of bias that seeps into the text, clouding facts and bypassing the normal critical judgment of the reader.[7]

Successful as the news magazine has been, it has tended to truncate the role of the Washington correspondent. Cloaked in anonymity, lacking a real voice in the final decisions on the "slant" of his stories, he denies and abdicates responsibility for the product. For years a mythical editor on the masthead of *Time* has been assigned blame when readers pointed out errors that have cropped up in a basically irresponsible system. *Newsweek* carries irresponsibility one step further in its Periscope columns, which are composed largely of stray rumors submitted by nonstaff contributors. The average Periscope item comes from a reporter who would not think of publishing it under his own name.

The sad aspect of the situation is that the news magazine

[7] Ben E. Bagdikian series in the Providence *Journal-Bulletin,* October 1958.

purveyed to its mass audience should have developed more rather than less responsible standards of journalism. The very power of these establishments gives added danger to their practice. For millions the processed facts represent the main contact with important national and international events. Despite the high abilities of many of the reporters, what comes out is often a deliberately doctored narrative, the more sinister because it is subtle.

❦ ❦ ❦

Television's arrival on the Washington scene brought more technicians than reporters. For the most part, the radio reporters moved into the new medium, joined by a number of former commercial announcers who showed the necessary dramatic talents. But the more widespread effect, once the camera entered such sanctums as the White House press conference, has been to make unpaid actors of the entire Washington press corps. Reporters now vie to ask questions simply to get themselves and the papers they represent in the limelight.

Television has singled out a few for more enduring fame. These are the reporters who are chosen to appear on the weekly interview programs from Washington. They must meet strange new criteria. Outstanding journalists in the capital have failed to make the grade while less able scribes have acquired nation-wide reputations. The premium is on the trigger-sharp tongue and the sneering manner of interrogation. It has created the public image of the Washington correspondent as a frustrated district attorney.

Television has contributed less than radio in adding dimension to reporting from Washington. The fifteen-minute nightly news show, originating in New York, presents more fragmentary news than the radio roundup, much of it chosen for eye interest rather than any genuine significance. The televised excerpts of the President's press conference, despite the networks' early zeal, are transmitted in the same fragmentary way. Attempts at reporting which could exploit the truly enormous potential of television have so far languished for want of a format or a sponsor.

So far television has shown no disposition to develop independent and fearless commentators who will carry on the tradition Elmer Davis and others brought to radio. It is not for lack of suitable candidates. High costs and the overriding urge to appeal to the mass audience have produced a cowardice among network executives in approaching issues that might be considered "controversial." The telecaster in Washington is keenly aware that he must work within rigid limits.

Perhaps the most biting indictment of the new media was made by leading telecaster Edward R. Murrow. "We are currently wealthy, fit, comfortable and complacent. We have a currently built-in allergy to unpleasant or disturbing information. Our mass media reflect this. But unless we get up off our fat surpluses and recognize that television in the main is being used to distract, delude, amuse, and insult us, then television and those who finance it, those who look at it and those who work at it, may see a totally different picture too late." Murrow bitterly castigates the practice of relegating the occasional informative program to the "intellectual ghetto" on Sunday afternoons. "For surely we shall pay for using this most powerful instrument of communication to insulate the citizenry from the hard and demanding reality which must be faced if we are to survive." [8]

The problem is the more serious, for television misused constitutes not simply a negative but a positive threat to the

[8] A speech delivered before the Radio and Television News Directors' Association in Chicago, October 15, 1958.

conduct of orderly government. Fragmentary reporting in this medium, even more than in printed journalism, tends to stimulate the staging of synthetic dramas. The politician cynical enough to fake an exhibition of histrionics manages to steal the few seconds of the nightly TV news roundup from the politician who has contributed sense to the public dialogue.

Television's influence on the behavior patterns of the congressional committee investigations has already been notable. Yet the network cannot resolve its dilemma simply by transmitting, as it has done on selected occasions, the full-length version of the hearings. This is an abdication of the reporting function. It makes the citizen himself take the place of the reporter in monitoring the conduct of government.

⁄ ⁄ ⁄

During the height of McCarthy's assault on the State Department, Secretary of State Acheson made a bitter declaration to the American Society of Newspaper Editors, "Now I don't ask you for sympathy. I don't ask you for help. You are in a worse situation than I am. I and my associates are only the intended victims of this mad and vicious aberration. But you, unhappily — you by reason of your calling — are participants. You are unwilling participants, but nevertheless, participants. And your position is far more serious than mine."

The McCarthy era came as a deeply unsettling experience to many Washington correspondents. The demagogue has been defined as the undetected liar. Yet, all the elaborate reporting mechanisms of the press seemed unable to detect and to communicate the basic fact of McCarthy's lies. As McCarthyism mushroomed in the nation's capital, the public dialogue grew strangely distorted. Serious reporters understood that the press was adding to the distortion rather than helping to bring it into focus.

More than at any time in the past, this experience has led to re-examination of the fundamentals of reporting — to questioning of the iron-clad concepts that rule the so-called "objective" or "straight" reporter. "The job of the straight reporter," a wire-service editor once defined for me, "is to take the place of the spectator who is unable to be present. Like the spectator, he does not delve into motives or other side issues except as they become a part of the public record." Unfortunately, the spectator is a casual witness, usually bewildered by any unexpected event. The reporter who limits himself to this role becomes frequently an unwitting agent of confusion.

There has been rebellion against this worn-out concept. As Eric Sevareid wrote, "Our rigid formulae of so-called objectivity, beginning with the wire agency bulletins and reports — the warp and woof of what the papers print and the broadcasters voice — our flat, one-dimensional handling of news, have given the lie the same prominence and impact that truth is given; they have elevated the influence of fools to that of wise men; the ignorant to the level of the learned; the evil to the level of the good." [9]

William S. White also aimed a blow: ". . . Objectivity is sometimes taken to mean only a careful — indeed, a meticulous — measuring out of absolutely even-handed credit and blame to this man against that, or to this movement against another. The theory seems to be that all's fair — and nobody has been impermissibly subjective — so long as everybody and everything comes out even in the end. This has sometimes put a curious veil over great and harsh issues." [10]

[9] Wallace Carroll, "The Seven Deadly Virtues," *Nieman Reports,* July 1955.

[10] William S. White, "Trying to Find the Shape — If Any — of the News in Washington," *Harper's Magazine,* August 1958.

The trouble with "straight" reporting is that it attempts to deny the creative role the reporter plays in government. For it is a myth that even the most passionately objective reporter can be truly straight in translating the multiple events he covers into the staccato of the teletype. He must constantly make decisions — for good or bad.

Even technical aspects of news production raise their own problems so far as objectivity is concerned. Let us examine the account of a typical working day described by an able wire-service reporter whose beat has been Capitol Hill:

> A central fact of life for the wire service reporter in Washington is that there are a great many more afternoon than morning papers in the United States. This creates a problem because the early afternoon paper on the East Coast goes to press between 10 and 10:30 A.M. — before the "news development" of the day. It means the wire service reporter must engage in the basically phony operation of writing the "overnight" — a story composed the previous evening but giving the impression when it appears the next afternoon that it covers that day's events.
>
> Let's take as an example the day the Austrian Treaty came up in the Senate. The evening before, I prepared a story of which three quarters was mere "background" concerning the Treaty. In the progressive developments that followed, this part of the story remained untouched. But I had to have a "lead" for my overnight so I called on Senator Walter George, Chairman of the Foreign Relations Committee, and tried out an "angle" on him. Would there be any U. S. military aid for the Austrian army? George said, "No money. Only long term credits." That became my lead. I had fulfilled the necessary function of having a story that seemed to be part of the next day's news.
>
> Next day, when the Treaty came up for debate in the Senate it was my job to get some "top" on this story. Senator Sparkman led off for the supporters of the Treaty. He had in his speech a couple of newsy items though nothing worthy

of filing as a "bulletin." So I dictated a new lead and picked up the main body of the story from my overnight. I threw away the George lead because it was a phony one.

After Sparkman came Senator Jenner. He was vitriolic against the Treaty. It was close to 2:30 which meant the deadline for the late afternoon papers. Was he worth a lead? I thought "No" because he represented such a minute minority in the Senate. But that was where a matter of judgment entered.

Suddenly, Jenner made a nasty crack about Eisenhower which was certainly newsier than anything Sparkman had said. How should I handle it? In deciding problems like this, I always have to consider what the other wire service reporters covering the same story may be doing. I decided not to lead with Jenner, but instead to move his section of the story into the office as an "insert." (All my decisions are reviewable in the office where the editors may make a decision based on factors I know nothing about.) But the Jenner paragraph moved as an insert which meant that there was a slug on the A-wire "Insert — Austrian Treaty paragraph after 'it was said . . .' "

A little after 3:30 P.M. the Treaty was adopted. That automatically constituted a bulletin to be sent out immediately on the A-wire even though it was accepted by everybody as a foregone conclusion. So I wrote a third lead for that particular story and then it was time to write a completely new story for next day's A.M. papers.

But my job had not finished. The Treaty adoption bulletin had gone out too late to get into most of the East Coast afternoon papers except the big city ones like the *Philadelphia Evening Bulletin,* which has seven editions. I had to find a new angle for an overnight to be carried next day by those P.M.'s which failed to conclude the Treaty story.

They don't want to carry simply a day-old account of the debate. They want a "top" to the news. So, to put it quite bluntly, I went and got Senator Thye to say that Jenner by his actions was weakening the President's authority. Actually, the Thye charge was more lively news than the passage of the Austrian Treaty itself. It revealed conflict among the Senate Republicans. But the story had developed out of my need for a new peg for the news. It was not spontaneous on Thye's part. I had called seven other Senators before I could get someone to make a statement on Jenner. There is a fair criticism, I recognize, to be made of this practice. These Senators didn't call me. I called them. I, in a sense, generated the news. The reporter's imagination brought the Senator's thinking to bear on alternatives that he might not have thought of by himself.

This can be a very pervasive practice. One wire service reporter hounded Senator George daily on the foreign trade question until he finally got George to make the suggestion that Japan should trade with Red China as an alternative to dumping its textiles on the American market. Then the reporter went straightway to Senator Knowland to get him to knock down the suggestion. It made a good story, and it also stimulated a minor policy debate that might not have got started otherwise. The "overnight" is the greatest single field for exploratory reporting for the wire services. It is what might be called "milking the news."

Of course, there are a great many other problems for the wire service reporter when he is covering a continuing story. Take, for example, the Reciprocal Trade fight which may go on for days or weeks. How many times do you play the anti-trade versus the pro-trade forces in the lead? These and many other factors enter one's realm of consciousness at a time when one is producing these stories at white hot speed.

There is also the problem of packaging. Our job is to report the news but it is also to keep a steady flow of news coming forward. Every Saturday morning, for example, we visit the Congressional leaders. We could write all the stories that we get out of these conferences for the Sunday A.M.'s but we don't. We learn to schedule them in order to space them out over Sunday's and Monday's papers.[11]

[11] Based on a confidential interview.

The point of this description, it seems to me, is to indicate just how complex the business of reporting really is. The phantasmagorial procession of straight news can itself produce a departure from true "objectivity." Within the routines that govern the straight reporter there is abundant room for bias to enter. Unless he makes reasonable choices, complex and long-drawn-out issues become progressively more distorted. He finds himself granting the forces of confusion greater access to the loudspeaker system of the press than the forces of clarity. McCarthy proved just how pliant such objectivity can be in the hands of the skilled manipulator.

The answer is not to impose ever more rigid strictures of objectivity on the reporter. Nor is it to go to the other extreme and revert to the loose pamphleteering traditions of early American journalism. The answer cannot be found in placing more and more emphasis on the packaging rather than the content of the news. Instead, there is need to recognize the reporter's proper role and responsibility in Washington. He is indispensable to the American system of government. He cannot be made to wear blinders. Rather he must be allowed to contribute an added dimension to reporting which is interpretive not editorial journalism.

In an age of big government, there must, of course, be ever greater reliance on team work and specialization among the press corps. But there are limits to composite journalism. Big bureaus servicing mass-communication media do not lessen the job of the individual reporter. He must be given time and incentive to delve deeply into complex issues. His importance today is greater than ever. His role in our republic requires every bit as much dedication and high sense of duty as that of the scientist, the soldier, or the statesman.

6

Intelligence and Counterintelligence

Part I

The Unending Fight against Secrecy

By conservative estimate 90 per cent of the important problems arising between the government and the press in Washington lie in that shadowy no-man's land of news ahead of the public event. This unending quest for what is variously called "background reporting," the "news behind the news," and "inside dope" engages the highest talent of the Washington correspondent. It is frequently a source of bafflement to the public official. Senator Robert Taft used to complain bitterly that reporters in Washington were so busy trying to find out what was going to happen that they did not provide a decent account of what had already happened.

The journalist explains his preoccupation in lofty terms. It is his job "to relate yesterday's fact to today's news to produce tomorrow's meaning.[1] His highest calling is "to prepare the public for what is going to happen next." [2] And, in more down to earth terms, "The power of the executive to decide things in secret is growing all the time . . . What reporters

[1] Roscoe Drummond.
[2] Walter Lippmann.

have to do now is move in much earlier in the development of policy. Of course, we've got to demonstrate a sense of history and give some guidance to the news, not just stick our finger in the President's eye. But if there is any big weakness in the press, it's not being aggressive enough. Never before has there been such a need for aggressive reporting during the drafting process so that there can be debate before it is too late." [3]

The struggle of the government's need for secrecy versus the public's right to know and the press's duty to find out and tell is unending. Too frequently it is discussed in public print in connection with the misguided efforts of a bureaucrat to cover up stupidity or wrongdoing. It deserves more serious consideration for it raises fundamental questions about government-press relations in a time of international peril — a condition likely to continue for the indefinite future.

In May 1955, Robert Cutler, who served for a long time as Special Assistant to President Eisenhower on National Security Council matters, spoke to a group of his fellow Harvard alumni on the subject, "Some Considerations Affecting the Publication of Security Information in Time of Propaganda War." In what is probably the most cogently reasoned statement of the case for secrecy ever made by a responsible government official, Cutler begins by defining security information. It includes "all the vast paraphernalia that goes into executive decision-making, and is imbedded in executive decisions, in the field of national security." A more precise definition, he argues, is no more possible "than it is possible to define the bounds of a fluid square foot in a rapid river."

Cutler then outlines some factors affecting the government's judgment in deciding what to make public: "the

[3] James Reston quoted by Joe Kraft in "Washington's Most Powerful Reporter," *Esquire,* November 1958.

nature of the opponent," "the nature of the opponent's warfare," "the skillful use of diplomacy," "the infinite complication of today's decision-making." As one who has sat in the nation's highest strategy council, he makes a fervent plea that strategic decisions must be reached as a result of a careful preparatory process — "In this acid bath all points of view are represented, heard, explored, and fought out."

Cutler asks, "Now in this long preparatory process . . . are the propagandists of one view or another to be given an opportunity to argue the pros and cons in the press?" He answers an emphatic no. "In fact, any other concept would lead to chaos . . . America would soon have, not integrated policy, but disintegrated policy."

Cutler does not believe this secrecy does violence to democratic government. "Until the President has acted, until he has approved a policy recommendation made to him by the National Security Council, *nothing has happened* . . . A Chief Executive should have the right not to take the advice of principal advisers, appointed by him, without the penalty of public disclosure" (italics mine).

The Presidential Assistant, who subsequently returned to the White House for another tour of duty, adds a vigorous personal testament to this plea for secrecy.

> For the last two and one-quarter years I have lived close to eleven hours a day amidst the arduous process of policy formulation. I am convinced that leaks to the press of matters in a discussion stage, of working papers, or oral Council deliberations, of bits and pieces of the vast paraphernalia that goes into careful, reasoned, sensible policy-making, play into the enemy's hands. Publicized differences of view among the President's chief advisers afford a ruthless enemy the rarest of chances to make trouble — to drive a divisive wedge between friends, between counsellors, between allies. In the face of the Soviet will and power and fixed determination, to give such a chance is to flirt with survival.

But Cutler is not prepared to rest his case at this point, for he proceeds to consider "the effect of public dissemination of sensitive security information, *even after the Presidential decision has been taken*" (italics mine). "The world we live in today," he argues, "is a seamless web . . . A touch upon the fabric here or there and strands of its warp and woof everywhere are pulled out of place . . . Every action or non-action, every significant move, every pronouncement of American leadership has its impact on other nations and other peoples."

More specifically, he argues that "our national security programs, military and non-military — upon which we are spending fifty billions a year — are a seamless web. They intermingle, they integrate and fuse so as to defy and make perilous any attempt to separate and compartmentalize." Like most officials in Washington, Cutler fully appreciates the power of publicity to alter programs. "Perhaps the most potent argument against public disclosure of secret projects or of short-falls (which inevitably always exist) in any one aspect of our national defense is that such disclosure builds up a Potomac propaganda war to rectify that defect or over-finance that project. But if you devote larger resources to one area of national defense, you are apt to imbalance the rest."

In summation, Cutler gets to the heart of his argument with clear words:

> In this world, where freedom as never before struggles rawly for survival, what is the role of free speech and free press in the United States with respect to publication of secret security matters? Is it enough today merely to assert these great principles in order to enjoy the right of their exercise in these secret and sensitive areas? Or should free speech and free press here validate their right to be heard? I suggest that, in these areas, they must make clear how they will contribute to our survival; they must prove to us that

the widespread, public disclosure of our secret projects will make the free world stronger, and the neutrals better disposed; will rally the subject peoples, and will put the Communist regimes at disadvantage.

A few months after Mr. Cutler staked out his position on the need for governmental secrecy, a group of editors and reporters gathered before a congressional committee to discuss "Availability of Information from Federal Departments and Agencies." [4] They spoke in language no less categoric:

To me the most insidious and dangerous thing about this fight for freedom of information is that it goes on day after day . . . I do not think many of us yet have realized the enormous implication of a battle in the middle of the 20th century for people to have access to information about the activities of their own public service. The fact that we have to fight for it at all is a sort of disgrace.[5]

Our public servants tell us that a little secret government is all right and particularly so when they are involved. Yet we can no more have a little secret government than we can have a little freedom, a little justice, or a little morality.[6]

Freedom to inspect public records is the most important freedom we have. Without this freedom — freedom of speech, freedom of the press, and even democracy itself, becomes meaningless.[7]

The Public business is the public's business. Freedom of information is the just heritage of this people. Without it they have but changed their kings . . .

My point . . . is there can be no practical utilization of the right of freedom of speech and freedom of the press without access to something to talk about in print. The or-

[4] *Hearings before a Subcommittee of the Committee on Government Operations,* House of Representatives, 84th Congress, 1st Session, November 7, 1955.

[5] James S. Pope, Executive Editor, Louisville *Courier-Journal.*

[6] V. M. Newton, Jr., Managing Editor, Tampa *Morning Tribune.*

[7] Clark Mollenhoff, reporter, Minneapolis *Tribune* and other papers. (This particular quote comes from a speech made on another occasion by Mr. Mollenhoff.)

gans of expression, the human voice, and the printing press, are silenced if information for them to operate with are withheld . . .

The people, in our American democracy, have a Constitutional right to factual information concerning the plans, policies, and actions of their Government. The burden of proof as to the need for withholding this information should, by every basic American principle, rest upon the agency or official who is determined to hold back the facts.[8]

James Reston outlined the problem in its most political terms:

It is true that the Government now has new problems. For example, when I first came to this town Mr. Hull would have press conferences every day, when we would ask him for information about what was going on in the Government prior to, say, a negotiation or prior to the presentation of a treaty to the Senate. He would tell us very properly to stay out of that. When the treaty went to the Senate, we would be able, as the Senate would, to criticize the treaty, to make any suggestions about it we would like, and report all of the facts about it. But now that this country is a member of a coalition, a total different sequence of events takes place. First of all, you have long and serious arguments within the executive branch of the Government to try to get a Government position to reconcile the differences concerning departmental policy. And in this phase, which sometimes goes on for months, we are told that we must stay out of this; this is not a proper area for enterprise by the press.

Then if it is a foreign-policy matter, and very few things are not these days, you go through a second stage, and that is the stage of trying to reconcile the American Government position with the position of all of our allies in the coalition. This sometimes goes on for many months. And again we are asked not to intrude into the policy-making, the policy-de-

[8] Harold L. Cross, Freedom of Information Counsel for the American Society of Newspaper Editors.

fining position; and, finally, when there is both a Government position and a coalition position, the paper is sent to the Senate, and they say, "For God's sake, do not touch this; it has taken us years to negotiate it out."

Now, I think that is a very serious — not just a newspaper problem — but it is a very serious national problem.[9]

✓ ✓ ✓

The battle over uncontrolled slippage of government secrets into print has been waged repeatedly in recent years. A junior official in the Department of Defense expressed the sense of frustration felt by some dealing in military secrecy: "At each day's end, I, along with many other officials of the Department of Defense, carefully lock my classified working papers in a safe that is in turn doublechecked by a colleague and triplechecked by a night security guard. More than once, I have come home to find the same kind of information I had just locked away detailed in my evening newspaper or a magazine." [10]

Both of the postwar Presidents have joined in the complaint. President Truman once claimed that "ninety-five per cent of our secret information has been published by newspapers and slick magazines," and argued that newsmen should withhold some information even when it has been made available to them by authorized government sources. President Eisenhower, in 1955, told a press conference, "For some two years and three months I have been plagued by inexplicable undiscovered leaks in this Government." He said that "technical military secrets" of value to Russia had been made public. Secretary of Defense Charles E. Wilson

[9] *Hearings before a Subcommittee of the Com. on Govt. Operations,* November 7, 1955.

[10] Murray Green, "Intelligence on a Silver Platter," in *The Reporter,* May 19, 1955.

estimated that this country was giving away military secrets to the Soviets that would be worth hundreds of millions of dollars if we could learn the same type from them.

To buttress the argument of American vulnerability, advocates of security tell of a Pentagon report on espionage during the Second World War known as "The Case of the Scholarly Spy." It concerns a German, sent to the United States in 1940, who instead of pursuing more spylike occupations spent much of his time studying the *New York Times Index* and the *Readers' Guide to Periodical Literature.* With this assistance, he collected several trunkfuls of data culled from major national publications. Returning to Germany in 1941, he prepared a report on "United States Air Armament" which ultimately fell into the hands of American intelligence agents. He had predicted American military aircraft production for the years 1941–1943 more accurately than had William S. Knudsen and T. P. Wright of the U.S. War Production Board.

A more contemporary horror story concerns an American engineer, untrained in intelligence methods, who decided to learn what he could about the U.S. guided missile program while waiting for government security clearance. By diligent reading in his public library, he compiled a forty-five-page report giving information on our arsenal of missiles — name, model designation, manufacturer, guidance system, method of propulsion, length, diameter, range, and altitudes. The report was so accurate that it was promptly classified.

ɻ ɻ ɻ

The battle between government secrecy and press intelligence grew deadly earnest in September 1951, when President Truman issued Executive Order #10290 extending "minimum standards" for handling security information to all Executive agencies of the government. A convention of the Associated Press Managing Editors Association, meeting in San Francisco, denounced the order as "a dangerous instrument of news suppression." When a deputation of editors called on Truman to protest, he requested them to make constructive suggestions for improving the Executive Order. The Association declined to undertake any such task, arguing that the order itself "erects dangerous barriers between the people and their Government."

There was approval from the press when the Eisenhower Administration substantially modified the Truman order, limiting the number of agencies dealing in classified information and eliminating the lowest classification "restricted" altogether. But before long new causes for dismay were discovered. It seemed that President Eisenhower was not simply concerned about the information being released to the press but about the extent to which it was publicized. According to one report of his thinking, he recognized that many items of information become known to Soviet technicians but are buried in their reports and fail to influence top leaders of the U.S.S.R. When, however, the same information is widely publicized and commented on by the American press, it acquires political significance and jogs the Soviet leaders into action.[11]

Approaching the security problem from a fresh angle, the Eisenhower Administration established an Office of Strategic Information in the Commerce Department. Soon it

[11] Walter Kerr, story in the New York *Herald Tribune,* June 1955. Chalmers Roberts, of the Washington *Post and Times-Herald,* recorded an instance in which a journalistic dispatch similarly jogged the thinking of one of the Western leaders: "Last spring Winston Churchill read a dispatch in the *Manchester Guardian* by its Washington correspondent, Max Freedman, about Rep. W. Sterling Cole's speech on the 1952 'hydrogen device' blast that 'obliterated the test island.' That newspaper account did something to the Prime Minister that no document could, and it brought him to Washington last summer to discuss the nuclear dilemma." (*The Reporter,* December 16, 1954.)

distributed to government officials a "balance sheet" which they were to apply in deciding "whether dissemination of information will help or harm the interests of the United States, in net balance, all things considered." The official was to weigh each item of potential news for: "Net effect" on military power, industrial power, morale and "other strategic angles." The Defense Department followed with a directive requiring its officers to determine whether information to be released would constitute, *"a constructive contribution to the primary mission* of the Department of Defense" (italics mine).

Great shouts of protest went up from the editors over these new attempts to control information. They claimed that their fears were abundantly justified a short time later when Secretary of Defense Wilson ordered Army Chief of Staff Matthew Ridgway's retirement letter withheld from the press. Wilson told reporters he put the "confidential" stamp on this unclassified document because he did not wish to add in any way to the problems of President Eisenhower and of Secretary of State Dulles at the Geneva Conference then taking place. The letter leaked to the press anyway.

✓ ✓ ✓

For the Washington reporter there is a note of unreality about much of the outcry over security and secrecy. He feels that it fails to get at the heart of the matter — the method and the motivation for the leakage of secret information to the press. Comparatively little of the traffic is in classified documents. The stuff of the news is not composed of such documentation. The Alsop brothers, who have disclosed more than their share of secrets over the years, claim that neither one has read a classified document since 1947. "Furthermore, if anyone now made us a present of a classified document," they have testified, "we should reject it as firmly as we should reject a pot of poison." [12]

How does the press acquire its secrets? The techniques of the "scoop" in this field are varied. First of all, the astute reporter learns a good deal by intuition. He reflects quietly on the processes that must be going on within the government in response to a given situation. Senator Paul Douglas once likened this cerebration to the explanation by the idiot boy of how he found the stray blind horse. "I shut my eyes and asked myself where I'd go if I were a blind horse; I went, and the horse was there."

The reporter follows his hunches, picks up a piece of the story here, another piece there. He plays one source off against another. Soon the pattern of a story — not necessarily the complete story — begins to emerge. In this field of projective analysis, James Reston has few peers. The details of the way he broke the news of the thirty-day Korean Armistice Plan in 1951 illustrates his technique:

> Last fall [Reston] began to feel disturbed about some background aspects of our negotiations. First there was the endless bickering over Kaesong, which seemed to him a trivial point. Then there were some leaks at the Pentagon about the strategic disadvantages involved in signing a truce, emphasizing, for example, the fact that Chinese armies would be released for operations in Southeast Asia. Next came Colonel Hanley's statement about the massacres of American prisoners. And finally, Acheson, who was in Paris, made what seemed to Reston a maladroit talk calling the Chinese "sub-barbarians." With this circumstantial evidence at hand, Reston began calling on the embassies of some of the UN countries with troops in Korea, expecting to find them skeptical of U. S. sincerity in the truce negotiations. "I turned out to be wrong," he recalled later. "When I took my suspicions to the embassies, I found out that some kind of plan was in the

[12] Joseph and Stewart Alsop, *The Reporter's Trade* (New York, 1958).

works. Then I was able to get a confirmation at the Department — so I got a one day beat." [13]

Part of the technique comes from a reporter's sense of timing — the calculation of the exact moment when pressure applied at a precise point in the government will yield results. The late Anthony Leviero, of the *New York Times,* revealed extraordinary talents in this. His exclusive story giving details of the Truman-MacArthur conference on Wake Island in 1951 was a case in point. Leviero has left a first-person description of how he got this story:

> It is not possible to tell all details of how the Wake Island story was obtained. It has to be done with some gobbledegook as to sources. On a rented television set on April 19, we watched and listened in the bureau office as MacArthur spoke before Congress. It soon became obvious that the speech would have a terrific impact and when it was over I said to Luther Huston that the country seemed to have forgotten that Truman and MacArthur had met at Wake and were supposed to have agreed on almost everything.
>
> I said I thought I ought to go after the Wake Island conference report. Huston told me to go ahead. (This disposes of the stories about a "plant," although I or any other Washington correspondent would gladly accept a planted authentic document.)
>
> I put in a call to source No. 1; he was out. Source No. 2 was in a conference, and that was also the story on source No. 3. I left a message in each instance and then it was a matter of waiting. The numbers have no significance as to the importance of the sources; they merely indicate the order in which they were called . . .
>
> All afternoon I monitored my telephone and if I went to the men's room I told the switchboard girl that if anybody called to keep him on the wire until I returned. No. 3 called back first, after 7 P.M. I put the proposition to him that per-

[13] From "The Troubled Press," in *Fortune,* February 1952.

haps now was the time to tell the story of the Wake conference. I said I would have to see the whole story and promised to use discretion in covering up my method of obtaining it.

No. 3 promised to see what he could do, as he had to go to higher authority. About an hour later No. 1 called. I told him the proposition I had made to No. 3 and asked his support if he saw fit. At 11 P.M., while still in the office doing a Sunday story, No. 3 called and I told him what I had told No. 1.

When I arrived at the office at 11 A.M. next morning I found an urgent message to call home. Having just moved into a house, I could only think that the boiler had exploded, or the roof caved in. But Mrs. Leviero said that No. 3 had called to say that I should call No. 2.

No. 2 told me to come to such-and-such place at noon. I filled two fountain pens and went. He put the source material before me in its original authenticated form. I horrified him by asking if I could use a typewriter. So I used the pens, using up one and part of the other in two hours of feverish scribbling. I had lunch and returned to the office, my arm still numb with writer's cramp.

A final word on the claims of discomfited rivals that this was an Administration "plant." Without conceding the story came from the White House, I can say that never in more than three years of covering the place did a member of the President's staff offer me a story. But I often scored by asking at the right time. I believe that at least a dozen reporters for rival newspapers, if they had figured out the prevailing mood of Administration sources that day and made the right approach, could have had the story.[14]

But the reporter's intuition and sense of timing are only one side of the business of transmitting the secrets of government. Leviero would never have got his story if a government official had not decided to provide him the information.

[14] Anthony Leviero, "Wide Awake on Wake," in *Times Talk,* May 1951.

What causes the leak? One veteran reporter has written, "The leak or exclusive story is rarely an example of a reporter's persistence and skill. More often it is simply an evidence of the harassed necessity of some official to put a situation before the public with a spurious sense of drama in order to gain attention for it." [15] On occasion, of course, human frailties — vanity, desire for vengeance or recognition — have led an official to disclose secrets that he ought not to have. But the primary cause for the almost constant revelation of behind-the-scenes episodes of government is the power struggle that goes on within the government itself or among the governments doing business in Washington.

On matters of foreign policy, the correspondent finds the foreign embassy in Washington is often a good peephole on what is happening behind the closed doors of the State Department. The embassy is not bound by purely American classifications about what is secret and what is not. But leakage does not end with the embassies. On national security matters, secrecy is repeatedly violated in the conflict among the great rival subgovernments in Washington — Air Force *vs.* Army *vs.* Navy; State *vs.* Treasury *vs.* Defense *vs.* the numberless special agencies and special assistants dealing in security matters. And, of course, there is the constant conflict between the Executive and Congress. These are not petty disputes. They represent the clash of major issues and ideas concerning the fate of the nation. Measured against the penalties incurred by a violation of secrecy, the benefits to be gained from publicity are at times irresistible to the partisans.

The realistic analysis of the situation reveals just how futile the absolutist position taken by Mr. Cutler really is. Our system of government itself operates to nullify the

[15] William S. White, "Trying to Find the Shape — If Any — of the News in Washington," in *Harper's Magazine,* August 1958.

"seamless web" of security he so ardently advocates. Much as he might wish to make it so, the National Security Council does not constitute a single orderly channel through which the high policies of government must flow before decisions are made. Important decisions are constantly being made all along the line. Frequently policies depend for their life or death on the publicity that can insure the public support and the funds from Congress to make them operable. Conversely, vital policies can be killed without trial or verdict by the National Security Council simply because of failures of publicity.

This is the way our government works and will likely continue to work even in a time of national peril. The misguided official who attempts to clamp an iron-handed control on the flow of information is doomed to frustration. Congress, far from tightening the laws on secrecy, has been more disposed to investigate and expose excessive security imposed by the Executive departments. A more fruitful course for government would be to consider how the flow of information may be better timed and coordinated so that the public receives a balanced story. Too often the real damage caused by public disclosures comes from the fact that the information is partial and biased.

On the other hand, the serious observer on the Washington scene must agree that certain secrets should be kept secret for at least a calculated interval of time. It is possible by premature publicity to disrupt the whole process of policy formulation. Particularly during the preliminaries to diplomatic negotiation, it can be harmful to the country's interest for other governments to be tipped off in advance about our government's bargaining position. Sometimes even the method in which a story is broken can be disastrous. The United Press's sensational disclosure of "Fail Safe," the story of our Strategic Air Command's operations in the Arctic, was a case in point. It should have been possible to describe our military precautions without resorting to the phony dramatics about bombers headed toward Moscow which alarmed our allies and provided propaganda material for the Soviets.

From time to time members of the press and government alike have come up with proposals for boards of impartial umpires to pass judgment on the more serious clashes over secrecy. Its powers could be limited. Indeed, the punishment of public censure ought to be adequate enforcement authority for a board sufficiently prestigious and unprejudiced. It would go a long way toward curtailing the excesses of secrecy in the government and sensationalism in the press.

Despite the various proposals for a public monitor in this field nothing has ever come of it. James V. Forrestal, the first Secretary of Defense, gave long and serious consideration to the problem. He felt that a system could be made to work if a government advisory committee could be established that the press and public would accept as "above self-serving." But, according to a newspaperman who knew him well, "Forrestal never could envisage a committee with that acceptance in peacetime." [16] It is a sad and sobering thought that Forrestal may well have been right.

[16] Arthur Krock, in the *New York Times,* July 2, 1957.

7

Intelligence and Counterintelligence

Part II

A Disquisition on Leaking

IN WASHINGTON it is always embarrassing when the lid blows off a story that was meant to be strictly "not for attribution." Like the small-town gambler who gets word from the police department that the heat is on, the reporter knows that for some unpredictable time there are going to be slim pickings in the vicinity. His job of reporting the news behind the news is going to be made a great deal more difficult.

For the government official, it is no less embarrassing. Not only have policies got caught and perhaps irredeemably mangled in the machinery of publicity; the official himself has been exposed in a practice which officialdom can never, never admit goes on. In all the literature of government, there is not one word on the technique of what has been variously called the "leak," or "cloaked news."

For the average citizen, who can be expected to bring only so much sophistication to the business of reading his newspaper, the problem is also serious. Unattributed news can be a highly confusing matter. Take, for example, one of the most notable instances of this practice. It happened during the spring of 1955 when there was one of the recurrent crises with the Chinese Reds over the islands in the Formosa Strait. On Saturday, March 26, the reader found a three-column thirty-six-point headline in the upper right-hand corner of page one in the *New York Times:* U. S. EXPECTS CHINESE REDS TO ATTACK ISLES IN APRIL; WEIGHS ALL OUT DEFENSE. Three days later, the reader found another headline in the same position, same type: EISENHOWER SEES NO WAR NOW OVER CHINESE ISLES.

If he studied the accompanying stories closely, he noted one similarity amid the contradictions. Neither had a single word to indicate who had presumed to speak in the first instance for the United States or in the second for President Eisenhower. The reader was obliged to take the word of the reporters, in these two instances highly reliable men, that their awesome stories were based on fact.

In point of fact, the source of the first story was Chief of Naval Operations Robert B. Carney, speaking to a select group of reporters at a background dinner. The second was none other than the White House press secretary, James Hagerty, who attended a hastily called second background conference in order to repudiate the stories arising out of the first.

During that particularly troublesome winter and spring, the citizen was obliged to accept a sizable quantity of news in this fashion. He was told that the evacuation of the Tachen Islands was a retrenchment designed to prevent a situation in which the Chinese Nationalists might involve us in fighting for some comparatively worthless real estate. Later he learned, via the headlines, that a "China Stalemate Foreseen by US in Formosa Policy" with a continuing situation of neither war nor peace. He was subsequently given lengthy and varying descriptions of the timing, the extent, and the conditions of potential war in the Far East, but always without being told who was making these life and death judgments. One newspaperman catalogued five basic contradictions in the stories emerging during a few days of late March 1955. It was truly a period of the background story gone wild.

But it was by no means a unique period. Cloaked news has become an institutional practice in the conduct of modern government in Washington, part of the regular intercourse between government and the press. During periods of high tension when formal channels of communication such as the President's and the Secretary of State's press conferences are cut off, it often becomes the major means by which important news is transmitted. In the words of one newspaperman describing the time of the Middle East crisis in 1956, "During the most critical period in recent months, at a time when any word out of Washington was considered of international significance, what had developed, it appeared, was government by leak."

✓ ✓ ✓

The leak in the form of selected news privately passed to a favored correspondent has an ancient history in Washington. In more recent times, Herbert Hoover, Sr., while still Secretary of Commerce, was an accomplished purveyor of these journalistic tidbits. The politicians and the brain trusters of the New Deal regularly used the leak as a method of launching trial balloons or waging intramural vendettas. President Roosevelt himself was known to have encouraged certain information to be slipped covertly to the press.

But it was not until the Second World War that the background briefing became a systematic practice. Two of the highest military officers, General George C. Marshall and Admiral Ernest J. King, instituted it by confiding to selected journalists some of the most delicate secrets of a nation at war.

As usual with affairs of the press, it began quite informally, almost haphazardly. Admiral King agreed to meet with a few reporters at a relative's home in Alexandria, Virginia. It was in early November 1942, a time when continued Japanese sinking of Navy ships was creating a national morale problem. King, though ordinarily a hardbitten and taciturn naval officer, came to enjoy these informal get togethers, and, according to one who attended, "learned to make use of the press with the skill of a public relations counsel." [1] An instance of this, King used the background conference to publicize and help nullify what he considered an ill-conceived plan to take General George C. Marshall away from his post as Army Chief of Staff.

For his briefings, General Marshall preferred the more austere surroundings of the conference room. But this didn't prevent him from making calculated revelations of great importance. At the time of the landing in North Africa, a noisy political uproar was developing because of General Eisenhower's dealings in Algiers with Admiral Darlan, of the Vichy Government. Marshall summoned thirty newspaper and radio men to his office. For nearly an hour he read to the assembled group Eisenhower's dispatches revealing all the details of the delicate diplomatic maneuvering. He had faith that the facts would dispel the rumors. It was all off-the-record, but soon the word spread around Washington and the Darlan scandal was cut down to size.

Marshall was utterly candid in these briefings, once disclosing to the reporters the Allied battle order in the West. It

[1] Lyle C. Wilson, "World War II," in *Dateline: Washington,* Cabell Phillips and Others, eds. (Garden City, N. Y., 1949).

was for their private information only; the reporters took no notes. After each session they usually compared recollections and prepared confidential memoranda for their editors. No one was expected to use what he learned there for a news story. The purpose of the briefings was largely preventative — to keep the reporter from going off half cocked. As Lyle C. Wilson, Chief of the United Press bureau in Washington has written, "This kind of access to the facts and to overall policy factors did not solve all the newsmen's problems of course. But it helped us to avoid going off on tangents of snap judgments, amateur opinion and plain peeve when the facts themselves could not be revealed to a puzzled public." In general, the system worked successfully during the war, although it did not answer the problem of what to do about the journalist who could not be accorded such trust.

✓ ✓ ✓

After the war, the practice of the background briefing expanded and flourished. Its main practitioners continued to be the veteran reporters from wartime Washington, but before long others were horning into the field. Some of the younger journalists went into competition by forming small quasi-social groups of their own for the purpose of dining and grilling the high and the mighty. Inclusion in the more intimate background sessions came to have prestige value in the journalists' caste system. Even the Press Association man, who earlier refused to consider a story without a solid quotable source, began to participate. Only such journalistic lone wolves as Drew Pearson and the Alsop brothers looked with disdain at these goings-on, preferring to gather their secrets by their own private contacts.

The ritual of these briefings is fairly uniform. On a specified evening, a dozen or so correspondents gather in one of the private dining rooms in the Metropolitan Club, or in a nearby downtown hotel. They are joined by the guest of honor, usually a high government official. It is not always clear who initiated the meeting. Usually, the official has graciously "responded" to a standing invitation to meet with the reporters. He may or may not wish to admit that he has something to disclose. Drinks are served and all sit down to dinner. Until this is completed, the conversation follows an aimless pattern. No one likes to appear eager. Then chairs are pushed back, the presiding correspondent raps on his glass, reminds his colleagues of the rules, and the session begins. Usually the official makes no formal remarks. He opens himself directly to questions from the correspondents. If he knows his business, he can always manage to steer things in the direction he wishes to move. Frequently, he does not openly admit that he is outlining a new government program or a drastic new approach to policy. He is merely "talking over" with the reporters some of the problems that confront him. He relies on them to have sense enough to grasp his meaning without having it spelled out for them. This studied casualness, at times, can breed misunderstanding and produce woeful consequences. The session sometimes goes on until quite late. Afterward, the chairman reminds everyone of the rules and each goes his separate way.

As the background briefings grew more frequent, the rules of the game also began to multiply and become more complex. Partly because the matters discussed at the conferences were not so delicate as during wartime, partly because the newsmen chafed at information purely for self-edification, there was an inevitable trend toward relaxing the strictures against publication. Now conferences may range from "deep" background to a variety of lighter hues, depending on the secretiveness of the informant. In the main, the so-called

Lindley Rule, first developed by Ernest K. Lindley of *Newsweek,* governs the proceedings. It requires, as has been noted, what amounts to compulsory plagiarism. The journalist may use what he has learned, but strictly on his own authority. Sometimes there are variations permitting him to quote "informed circles" or "a high government spokesman."

Usually there is at least one day's moratorium on the news coming out of such background briefings. If the news is especially hot, it may be arranged that nothing will be printed until the informant gets out of town, so that he can establish a convenient alibi. But nothing is hard and fast about the arrangements. Misunderstandings are frequent, increasing in direct ratio to the importance of the news.

The postwar uses of the background session have been varied. It has been a means of alerting the press to the gravity of a situation being overlooked in the news. Dean Acheson, while still Undersecretary of State, called in a small group of reporters and gave them the "background" on current Soviet demands against the Turks. It helped focus world attention on a situation of indirect aggression that could have grown much worse if it had not been publicized.

The background conference is also used in the attempt to allay press alarm. A dubious instance of this occurred when George Kennan, Chairman of the Policy Planning Board of the State Department, held one at the time of President Truman's announcement of Russia's atomic explosion. Contrary to the facts, Kennan assured reporters that the timing of the Soviet feat did not come as a surprise to American policy planners. He was deliberately trying to play down the story in an effort to avert hysteria among the American people.

For the official, this use of cloaked news as an indirect instrument of persuasion offers many attractions. John Foster Dulles, a regular practitioner of the art, more than once applied it to secure concessions from an ally. Shortly before the London conferences to negotiate the Japanese treaty, Dulles informed reporters for "background purposes" that the treaty was in a grave crisis. The resulting publicity brought tremendous pressure on the British even before they had sat down at the conference table to make the concessions Dulles wanted. Ironically, the British used the same kind of pressure on Mr. Dulles and his colleagues during the 1953 financial and economic conferences in Washington by leaking to certain reporters the story that only the President's intervention had saved the talks.

Most frequently the leak is symptomatic of rivalry in the higher echelons of the government itself. Harold E. Stassen, once Special Assistant to the President on disarmament questions, would hold a background conference to discuss modifying U. S. proposals for arms control. Promptly Secretary of State Dulles would hold his own background conference to "clarify" the news coming out of the Stassen conference.

Mr. Dulles has had the same behind-the-scenes repudiation of his policies. On December 7, 1956, the Washington *Post and Times-Herald* carried the headline: NEW AID TO EUROPE STUDIED: GOVERNMENT MAY REVISE HUGE GIFTS TO ITS ALLIES. The story emanated from a Metropolitan Club dinner reporters held with the Secretary of State. Two days later, the newspapers carried stories sponsored by an anonymous spokesman in the Treasury Department irritatedly disputing the Dulles proposition. The Treasury Department zealously attempts to plug all leaks that have anything to do with the spending of money.

The leak is traditionally used as a method of promoting a new program prior to its formal unveiling before Congress. In Great Britain, where the Cabinet has a strong obligation to report initially to the House of Commons, such use of the press to launch legislative programs would be unthinkable.[2] In Washington it is habitual. Prior to the announcement of the so-called "Eisenhower Doctrine" for the Middle East, Mr. Dulles engaged in three days of systematic leakage to the reporters on the details. By the third day, when congressional leaders were finally informed of the new proposal, one news dispatch noted that they "were cautious in their reaction . . . but the Administration's plan had been so widely publicized before the leaders reached the White House that . . . they can do little more than adopt the new policy as presented." [3]

The often sorely pressed Washington official sees numerous advantages to this system. It gives him a semi-anonymous voice in the cavernous echo chambers of the nation's capital. The responsible official, by keeping members of the press informed, can engage in preventative action against the thousand and one stories that crop up from nowhere and do damage to sound policy. In addition, it permits greater flexibility in taking policy initiatives. Without risking either his or his department's reputation, the official has a chance to take a measure of public — and more immediately important — congressional opinion. If opinion is hostile, he can always fall back on what has been called "the technique of denying the truth without actually lying."

This technique works as follows: Secretary Dulles, in 1953, held a background conference in which he revealed to reporters that he had been doing some tentative thinking about a Korean boundary settlement along the line of the narrow waist of the peninsula. The stories that emerged provoked

[2] During the Tribunal Inquiry into the Bank Rate leak in 1957, there was much speculation whether the Chancellor of the Exchequer had violated his obligation to report first to Parliament when he held a private session with several editors prior to announcing a rise in the bank rate. It turned out that he had told the editors nothing about the raising of the bank rate even though it would have been useful in promoting the mood of confidence he hoped to bring about.

[3] *New York Times,* January 1, 1957.

criticism on Capitol Hill, particularly from Senate Republican Leader William Knowland. Forthwith, there issued a White House denial, drafted by none other than Dulles himself, which stated that "the Administration has never reached any conclusion that a permanent division of Korea is desirable or feasible or consistent with the decisions of the United Nations."

The pertinent words of course were "conclusion" and "permanent." The White House statement was not, in fact, what it seemed — a clear repudiation of what Mr. Dulles told the reporters and what they wrote, perforce on their own authority, for their papers.

Yet, despite these ambiguities, cloaked news has at times played a creative part during the malleable period of policy formation. Historian Bruce Catton has concluded that "Our particular form of government wouldn't work without it." The critics — and there are a lonely few among the newsmen who stubbornly refuse to attend any news conference that is not on the record — make a number of arguments. They decry the informality that curses the whole practice. Mixing business and pleasure at the background dinner, with usually a goodly number of drinks thrown in, serves to befuddle the newsmen as well as the official. The reporter usually does not take notes while the official is present. (This might cramp the official's style.) Usually there is painful reconstruction afterward of what exactly was said. No one ever seems to be quite sure what the rules are.

An ironic instance of this occurred after the Hagerty conference repudiating Carney's leaks. Several of the newsmen, including Roscoe Drummond, Bureau Chief of the New York *Herald Tribune* and Lyle Wilson of the United Press, went home to bed thinking there would be the usual moratorium on this story. They were aroused from sleep a few hours later by anguished calls from their New York offices. They had been scooped by their more enterprising colleagues.

The responsible reporter and the official alike complain of some of the tendencies in reporting background news. Inevitably, it tends to harden the news and to give it a sound of finality that may not have been intended. Apparently Secretary Dulles was a victim of this when the stories coming out about the possible Korean boundary settlement were written with a flatness that he had not intended. Instead of gently floating a trial balloon, he discovered he had inadvertently launched a jet-propelled new policy. He felt obliged to shoot it down in self-defense.

The fault for this is not exclusively the reporter's. Because he cannot quote a source, he finds it almost impossible to convey in his story the subtle gradations of meaning that good reporting requires. The background briefing provides a field day for any colleague who prefers to present the news in stark, cataclysmic terms.

Inevitably, the case against cloaked news gets down to the fundamental concepts of reporting. What is the reporter's responsibility? Is he an intelligence agent for his paper and via it the American public? Or is he to be made a tool of the government's counterintelligence operations? Arthur M. Schlesinger, Jr., has posed the alternatives in fairly stark terms: "Washington newspapermen today hardly know whether to believe the Secretary of State, because they do not know if he is speaking to them as reporters or seeking to use them as instruments of psychological warfare . . . What is the responsibility of a newspaperman when he discovers that some rumored development of policy is really only a psychological warfare trick? Should he print the truth at the risk of wrecking the plans of the Secretary of State? Or should he suppress the truth, betray himself, and deceive the American people?" [4]

[4] Arthur M. Schlesinger, Jr., "Psychological Warfare: Can It Sell Freedom?" in *The Reporter*, March 31, 1953.

In this, as in much that concerns reporting in Washington, the absolutist position has little relevancy to the reporter's workaday world. He cannot narrowly demarcate his sphere of operations. He is caught and intimately involved in the ceaseless battle of intelligence versus counterintelligence. He can remove himself from the battlefield only at the risk of negating his role as a reporter.

A more fruitful inquiry may be directed into the conditions that should be imposed on cloaked news as a technique of communication. On the government's part, there needs to be a clearer recognition of the limits to which this practice can go. No matter how compelling the exigencies, the press in a free society should not be turned into the government's propaganda instrument. A fine line has to be drawn between the diplomatic and the deceitful. The government went over that line when, during the Quemoy-Matsu crisis of August 1958, Secretary Dulles issued a public statement of official policy, then immediately afterward proceeded to make more sweeping pronouncements to reporters on a not-for-attribution basis. He was transferring an unfair burden to the reporter.

The main responsibility in guarding against the misuse of counterintelligence, however, lies not with government but with the press. Just as government must take the initiative in safeguarding its essential secrets, so the reporter must in the first instance decide what is proper and what is improper practice in the handling of the leak.

There are good grounds for thoughtful review in this field. In his eagerness to get at the inside news, even the good reporter frequently loses the keen discrimination he shows in his more open reporting. As William S. White has written, "Often reporters handle a leaked story with a solemn uncriticalness. The documents, or whatever, are ceremoniously produced for the public — which at times must scratch its head in perplexity as to what the devil they are all about. The motivation for the leak usually is not mentioned, although that may be the most significant part of the story." [5]

One example of this: the reader needed to know in order to understand the Admiral Carney story that this attitude toward an inevitable war in Asia was nothing new on Carney's part. Indeed, after the fall of Dienbienphu ten months earlier, Carney had made a similar exhortation in a public speech, comparing the situation to that of Munich. No news story could have been complete without mentioning this long standing attitude of the man or the fact that others, even among the Joint Chiefs, disagreed with him. Instead, the sudden publication of the unattributed stories in many of the major newspapers made it look as if all official Washington had arrived simultaneously at the prediction of war.

The reporter is guilty of deceits in the business of cloaking the news. He refers vaguely to "informed circles" implying a plurality of opinion, when in fact he may be quoting the views of one person. He plays leaks with an importance they would not deserve if their sources were made known.

There is no reason why the rules for cloaked news cannot be made to fit the needs of honest reporting. For example, when anything of a highly controversial nature comes forth at a background session, the moratorium should be extended long enough to enable the reporter to check other sources. Few instances occur when anonymity need be carried to the point that the reporter must deliberately confuse his reader about what is being related. The reporter's first obligation is to present a clear and balanced story.

This war of intelligence *versus* counterintelligence is likely to remain one of the perplexing phenomena of the Washington scene. Though limits may be imposed on its excesses, there is no possibility of ever declaring a permanent truce. The conditions that give rise to it are basic to the Amer-

[5] In "News in Washington," *Harper's Magazine*, August 1958.

ican system of government and the free condition of American society. For the reporter, few hard and fast rules can be laid down to serve him as a permanent code of conduct. Instead he must be governed in his daily work by sound and subtle judgments. It is one more measure of the creative role he has to play in the political life of Washington.

8

Putting Government on the Spot: A Comparison in Interpellative Arrangements

> I think an analogy to [the Question Period] in Britain is our public press conference which the President faces, and at which he answers the same sort of questions he would answer if he were on the Floor of the Congress. I don't think it's practical under our system to have that take place in the Congress of the United States. George Washington tried it one time and he got so disgusted with the way they treated him that he went back to the White House and never went down there any more.
>
> HARRY S. TRUMAN*

QUITE REGULARLY nowadays the quick comparison is drawn between the press conferences held by the American President and his Cabinet members with the Question Period in the British House of Commons. This comparison needs to be examined, for the dissimilarities are numerous enough to obscure the common purpose of these two unique institutions, both aimed at putting government leaders on the spot.

Though the Question Period's lineage can be traced back to the seventeenth century when the first peer rose in the House of Lords to interrogate a Minister, it has been remarkably neglected as a subject of scholarly analysis. A search of

* CBS Television Program, "Small World," November 30, 1958.

the libraries in London revealed only one book devoted to the subject, and disappointingly this one only dealt with the questions which have been asked rather than with the Question Period as an institution playing such a central role in British government.[1] For Minister and ordinary Member of Parliament alike "questions" constitute an important and time-consuming business. Four days a week in the House of Commons, commencing directly after opening prayers at two-thirty in the afternoon, the Speaker takes up the printed Notice Paper listing the questions that have been filed for oral answer. The Question Period lasts until three-thirty and may by parliamentary maneuver even by stretched out a few minutes longer.

It is a time when the House seems to come alive. Members crowd into the small chamber, government and opposition confronting each other across the narrow aisleway. The Speaker, looking slightly archaic in his white wig, mounts the pulpit-like stand from which he presides. He calls *seriatum* the numbers from the Notice Paper whereupon both the Member presenting the question and the Minister to whom it is addressed promptly rise. There is no oral repetition of the question. The minister, standing behind the ancient dispatch box which serves as a lectern, reads the prepared answer from his portfolio. When he has finished, the Speaker calls on the Member, who may then address to the Minister what is known as a Supplementary. Others rise and seek recognition. At this point the dialogue grows more lively and less formal. Though marked by flowery references to "the Right Honorable Minister" and "the Honorable Member from ——," it departs from the prepared texts and depends entirely on the combatants' wit, acumen, and thorough knowledge of the subject at issue. After a suitable exchange, the Speaker calls out

[1] Patrick Howarth, *Questions in the House: The History of a Unique British Institution* (London, 1956).

the next number and the questioning moves on to a new subject and, perhaps, a different Minister.

For the free-wheeling Washington correspondent, there is much that appears dubious about this British institution. In the first place, only the elected representatives, principally Her Majesty's Loyal Opposition, ask the questions, while the press performs merely a recording function. Furthermore, there is a referee — unthinkable at the President's press conference — in the person of the Speaker. His decisions on procedure and admissibility of questions are governed by precedent and almost always are accepted as final. A Member of Parliament must post written notice of his question at least two days in advance. He is limited to three questions to which oral answers may be required. Although he is permitted a number of supplementaries, this is always at the discretion of the Speaker. His questions must be directed to the Minister primarily responsible for the particular matter, although the Prime Minister may be asked if the statement of a Cabinet Minister represents the policy of the Government.[2]

The mere listing of precedents in Sir Erskine May's official rule book of Parliament sounds excessively restrictive to those acquainted with American practice. Questions should relate to the "public affairs" with which Ministers are officially connected, either to matters pending in Parliament or to matters of administration for which they are responsible. An explanation can be sought regarding the intentions of the government but not an explanation of the Minister's opinion on matters of policy. An answer cannot be insisted upon if refused by the Minister on the ground of "the public interest." The purpose of a question is to obtain information or press for action, and it should not be in effect a short speech or framed so as to suggest its own answer or convey a particular

[2] Sir Thomas Erskine May, *The Law, Privilege, Proceedings and Usage of Parliament* (16th ed., London, 1957).

point of view. The facts on which a question is based may be set out briefly, *provided* the Member asking it makes himself responsible for their accuracy. In cases where the facts are sufficiently important, the Speaker has been known to request *prima facie* proof of their authenticity.

Unlike some press conferences in Washington, great care must be taken to protect reputations. A question which publicizes the names of persons or statements not strictly necessary to render the question intelligible will be refused a place on the Notice Paper. Introducing the names of persons or bodies invidiously or for the purpose of advertisement is strictly prohibited.

Questions which violate precedent may be rejected by the Recording Clerk or, when brought up in the House, disavowed by the Speaker. Among the examples of those judged inadmissible, May cites the following: asking for the solution of a hypothetical proposition; seeking, for purposes of argument, information on matters of past history; raising questions of policy too large to be dealt with in the limits of an answer to a question; repeating in substance questions already answered or to which an answer has been refused; being trivial, vague or meaningless. The Speaker has also requested that questions on purely local matters or dealing with individual cases should be turned over for printed answer.

The Washington correspondent, pondering the exclusion of questions of a type that regularly come up at the White House, might wonder what there is possibly left to ask. Isn't the Question Period too hedged about with restrictions to be of any great value? The answer, as any observer in the House of Commons can testify, is decidedly in the negative. It is impossible to attend the Question Period day after day without becoming acutely aware of its vital role in keeping British government responsive and responsible.

In periods of crisis, domestic or foreign, an almost electric feeling permeates the House during the Question Period and infects even the casual spectator. There is the same sense of testing that engages the *aficionado* of the bull ring, only in this case it is mind being pitted against mind rather than man against beast. There is the feeling that at any moment the best prepared plans of the government may go awry. The game is being played before an attentive audience — the other Members, whose roars of approval or disapproval rise or fade depending on the skill of the Minister in meeting the assault. Major policy battles have been won and lost during the Question Period. "Starting no bigger than a man's hand, any question may develop into a crackling, intense storm, with thunder and lightning, and may even lead beyond the question hour into a full debate on Government policy on a later day. There is a contingent, tense relationship, a kind of menace underneath the purring, which is exciting for the lions, the gladiators, and for the public. There is real mental strife." [3]

The Cabinet Minister finds here a major measure of his leadership. Amid the competing hoots and *hear, hear*'s, he and his colleagues receive judgment for a job well or poorly done. The pace is lightning fast, at times almost too rapid for the unaccustomed ear of the American spectator. Amid such crossfire, neither interrogator nor interrogatee can rely absolutely on the prepared statement. The object is by a clash of wit to expose the raw undersides of policy. It is for the Minister a serious and, moreover, a continuous ordeal. "He might get by with an evasion on Monday, but he is in the ring again on Tuesday. He may be witty and escape in a gust of laughter on Wednesday, but the questions may trip him on Thursday. He cannot escape all the questions all the time." [4]

[3] Herman Finer, *The Theory and Practice of Modern Government* (New York, 1950).

[4] Finer, *Theory and Practice.*

The ordeal is communicated vicariously to the underlings in the Minister's department. "The question hour . . . is dreaded more than any other hour by the Civil servants, and it keeps them up to the mark much better than any other way which anybody could suggest." [5] In the Ministry of Housing and Local Government, for example, a new file is opened for every Parliamentary question and on the covers of these files are to be found the words: "To be dealt with *IMMEDIATELY* and not placed with other papers." [6]

For the up and coming member of the opposition, the Question Period offers a prime opportunity to display prowess in putting Her Majesty's Ministers on the spot. The phrasing of the Supplementary is one of his more assiduously practiced arts. He does well to nourish whatever gift he may have in this verbal crossfire. More than one British leader has risen to prominence by means of the reputation acquired during the Question Period. An acid-tongued Welshman named Aneurin Bevan first won fame when he rose in the House to hurl a challenging question at Winston Churchill and, to the surprise of everyone, managed to best the redoubtable Prime Minister in the furious exchange that followed.

There have been criticisms of this remarkable institution. It tends, say the critics, to place too much emphasis on quick verbalizations rather than on sounder statesmanship. It provokes displays of wit which are not always truly revealing of the deeper questions at issue. The apocryphal story is told of the two Members who, being lost in an English fog, inquired of a farmer as to their whereabouts. He replied laconically, "You're in your car." The two Members agreed that this was an excellent Parliamentary answer since it was brief, it was true, and it "shed absolutely no light upon the situation."

[5] Sir Ivor Jennings, *Parliament* (2nd ed., Cambridge, Eng., 1957).
[6] Howarth, *Questions in the House.*

Viewed as an interpellative arrangement, however, the British institution bears a number of marked advantages over the American press conference. In London, the questions are asked by elected Members of Parliament who are politicians long trained in the art of government. Each one of them recognizes the possibility that some day he may be on the other side of the firing line as a Cabinet or sub-Cabinet Minister. Thus his questions, though perhaps highly partisan, are generally responsible. In Washington, the questioning is conducted according to the reporter's concept of what is news. He is, or is supposed to be, nonpartisan, but he is not always inclined to be responsible. He does not approach government as one who may someday be responsible for deciding policy himself.

The Parliamentary Question Period generally insures the opportunity to raise questions when policy is still in a fluid stage. Questions focus the issue while there is still time for the government to alter policies which do not stand up before criticism. Of course, the Minister can always decline "in the public interest" to answer. It is theoretically possible to ignore and even to deceive Members of the House. The British attack on Egypt in 1956 was planned by Prime Minister Anthony Eden without the knowledge of some of his own Cabinet Ministers. The discretionary power of a Prime Minister is immense. But on the very day Eden announced his Suez invasion, he was obliged to submit to merciless questioning in the House.

The Washington correspondent, on the other hand, may be put off for weeks during a period of crisis. No one compels the President to hold a press conference. Even when one is called reporters are sometimes frustrated by a presidential embargo on questions relating to an issue currently in a delicate state. Alternatively, they may be referred by the President to one of his department heads who may or may not be available for questioning.

It is doubtful whether a British Prime Minister could have continued for so many years to display the ambiguous position on a critical foreign policy issue that President Eisenhower showed toward the offshore islands in the Formosa Strait. Here was a case in which substantial members of the press and the opposition party felt serious qualms, but failed to develop an effective interpellative arrangement. The presidential "no comment" was quite final.

For the able Member of Parliament the supplementary question is more important than the original. He seeks out the chink in his opponent's armor and makes his thrust. He voices his incredulity with such sarcastic flourishes as "Does my Right Honorable Friend really mean . . . ?" or "Is my Right Honorable Friend aware that . . . ?" Should the Minister prove sufficiently mendacious, the Member can always attempt to take the matter into regular Parliamentary debate and, if the matter be serious enough, threaten to topple the government itself. The British Cabinet Minister thus feels a far reaching consequence to his responses.

The Washington correspondent has no such power of pursuit. Having survived the gymnastic contest necessary to gain recognition at the President's press conference, he finds it practically impossible to ask a follow-up. On occasion, when the valiant reporter has managed a supplementary question, he has been curtly dismissed for trying to monopolize the proceedings. Lesser officials, such as the Secretary of State, do, however, receive a more thorough going-over.

The American system of government, it is true, relies much more heavily than the British on legislative committee surveillance. Through the formally staged committee hearings and also the countless informal briefings, the Executive department endeavors to be responsive to congressional inquiries. At times, the constant interchange works very well indeed. At other times, as I have tried to indicate in Chapter 3, the publicity-seeking committee investigation can be destructive of Executive policy making.

Several factors hamper the congressional committee probe as an interpellative device. The committee chairman, who exercises vast discretionary power in all committee matters, attains his position solely through seniority. Sometimes a major committee can be crippled when it is needed most by the doddering old man at its helm. The chairman of the Senate Foreign Relations Committee until recently was a nonagenarian who took over from a late septuagenarian. There was a substantial decline in that Committee's effectiveness in reviewing United States foreign policy.

Most of the time the committee lacks the capacity to pose its questions to the Executive contemporaneously, i.e., while the policy at issue is still in a formative stage. There is endless opportunity to interrogate Cabinet members and civil servants before the drafting of legislation or in the preparation of money bills. But the committee cannot always confront a government leader at the time of a bold new policy initiative and examine publicly its implications. By and large, the Congressmen must be content with the post mortem — a procedure that usually does little to rectify past errors of judgment and may even by endless re-examination of *faits accomplis* serve to hamstring present judgment. U. S. policy toward China, for example, has not been notably improved by the constant inquiries into why China fell to the Communists in the first place.

The British penchant for the post mortem is not nearly so well developed as ours. Compared to the battalions of congressional committee investigators, select committees of the House of Commons operate with only a skeleton staff, usually a single clerk. They go about their business with a minimum of publicity. By comparison, the Opposition Party is highly reticent about calling for the review of past governmental blunders. After the policy on Suez had failed and had been altered, Labour Party leaders refrained from demanding a full inquiry into the decision to attack in the Middle East.

But the British on occasion are known to do a thorough job of searching out alleged abuses. When scandals arise that could be damaging to basic government institutions, they sometimes resort to an investigative arrangement known as the Tribunal of Inquiry. Its procedures might seem a bit unusual to the American Congressman. The three members usually chosen from the high court justices and eminent Queen's Counsels, are appointed by the very government whose conduct is being investigated. The Attorney General, himself a member of the Cabinet, takes charge of presenting the evidence, examining and cross-examining the witnesses. Members of the Opposition Party have no voice in the proceedings, except as they individually may be called upon to testify. The Inquiry could easily be dismissed as a rigged affair.

Yet these tribunal investigations proceed with a relentlessness that dispels all suspicion of partiality. In 1948, a Tribunal was appointed by the Labour Government to "inquire into allegations reflecting on the official conduct of Ministers of the Crown and other public servants." Under the merciless probing of the Labour Government's Attorney General, the Right Honorable Sir Hartley Shawcross, a senior political officer and several Civil Servants were obliged to resign because of their indiscretions.

In the fall of 1957, this reporter attended several sessions of a Tribunal of Inquiry investigating rumors that there had been advance disclosure when the Chancellor of the Exchequer boosted the bank rate from 5 per cent to 7 per cent. It had been alleged that some investors privately profited as the result of a leak. This was a most sensitive area to be investigated, since it involved backroom affairs of the financial establishment of England. Upon the belief in the integrity of this establishment rests the pound sterling and, for that matter, the British Commonwealth.

Several aspects of the Inquiry struck me as significant. First, it managed to avoid all the jurisdictional entanglements that often ensnarl a congressional inquiry into an Executive agency. Leading Cabinet Ministers, Civil Servants, and Directors of the Bank of England were haled before the Tribunal and made to testify about the intimate details of their conduct. No one refused to testify on grounds of executive privilege — a practice that frequently serves to frustrate a congressional committee and to foreclose major avenues of investigation. Even the journalists who had written stories alluding to "leaks" were called before the Tribunal, told to name their sources, and, under risk of contempt of court, ordered to comply. The questions put by the Attorney General, Sir Reginald Manningham-Buller, Q.C., and by the members of the Tribunal left very little unexplored.

Unlike Washington practice, those who raised the allegations were examined as severely as those against whom the allegations were raised. Harold Wilson, former President of the Board of Trade under the Labour Government, was made to defend every statement he had issued on the subject. In the stern atmosphere of the hearing room, presided over by three eminent jurists of the nation, there was little personal or political profit for those who loosely repeated unsustained charges.

The British press was obliged to handle the Inquiry with a caution unknown to journalists covering congressional committee probes. The leading newspapers carried each day a lengthy paraphrase of the testimony. But any attempt of an editor to draw conclusions about the meaning of the testimony was sternly rebuked by the Tribunal. Two newspapers that went astray were publicly criticized by the Attorney General for their indiscretions and threatened with contempt charges. In one instance, the editor hurried down from Scotland to apologize for a misleading headline.

The inquiry having been conducted in a nonpartisan and judicious atmosphere, the report presented by the Tribunal was clear and definitive. It left none of the unresolved doubts that sometimes linger on after the congressional inquiry, polluting the political atmosphere of Washington and undermining public confidence in government institutions. The Tribunal, having found that the allegations of a bank-rate leak were baseless, endorsed the hope expressed by the Governor of the Bank of England that ". . . everybody who has it in his power to remedy the damage which has been done by those rumours, will make every effort so to do, not least those persons who may have wittingly, or unwittingly, contributed to the circulation of those rumours." [7]

There is, of course, only limited usefulness in comparing British to American practice. The vast differences arise from two quite fundamentally different systems of government. In Britain, the undivided authority of government lies in Parliament. In America, authority is parceled among three separate and coordinate branches of government. No one branch is wholly accountable to the other two. As far back as Tocqueville, students of American government have been awed by the role that public opinion is daily called to play in order to make the system mesh at all.

In Britain, public opinion plays a lesser role in the daily conduct of government. One senses that the business of government is being carried on much more exclusively among the elected representatives of the people. As a direct consequence, the British press seldom ever bothers to "report" government with the thoroughness and persistence of the

[7] *Report of the Tribunal Appointed to Inquire into Allegations of Improper Disclosure of Information Relating to the Raising of the Bank Rate, Presented to Parliament by the Secretary of State for the Home Department by Command of Her Majesty, January 1958.*

better American press. As one British observer has remarked, "The ablest American newspapermen are reporters; the ablest British newspapermen are editorial writers."

In Washington, the press has moved naturally and inevitably to fill the gaps in the system. Reporters must perform the interpellative function that members of Congress are not allowed to perform. The press conferences of the President and the numerous other press institutions that have grown up as a way of putting government on the spot serve a very necessary purpose.

At their best, the reporters meet their responsibility quite well. There have been conferences with the Secretary of State and others during periods of crisis when the press revealed tremendous skill, knowledge, and determination to get to the heart of the matter. Week after week at the President's press conference, a small but powerful group of correspondents work hard to place the central issues before the nation's Chief Executive.

At other times the press bungles its job badly. Foolish or irresponsible reporters dominate the conferences. The equating of news with sensationalism distracts attention from grave problems at hand. The press rushes hell-bent after the trivial and the fleeting, ruled more by a compulsion to make headlines than to exercise its more serious calling. Government leaders are capable at times of evasions and even downright deceptions without being clearly exposed.

That is why it is useful to examine British institutions as a yardstick, if nothing more, for performance. With remarkable consistency they manage to keep the public dialogue relevant and responsible. They serve to bring issues into focus and to make government leaders anxious and answerable for their conduct. At the same time they refrain from probing the government in such a way as to do lasting damage.

In America, with increasing frequency as our world responsibilities have mounted, the public dialogue seems to grow distorted and unreal. When the times are really perilous, there is a tendency to abdicate discussion altogether. "One of the remarkable aspects of the Middle East crisis has been the comparative silence of the American people and the almost total lack of debate on the whole thing in Congress," a reporter commented during one tense point in that recurrent crisis.[8] A Congressman who ventured to discuss the issues was told by Speaker Rayburn that it was a good time to avoid public discussion.

The remarkable and alarming thing is how ephemeral the mighty publicity processes of our government can prove to be in moments of testing. Press conferences can be canceled. Inquiries can be abruptly postponed. Overnight and for an unspecified duration a great government can pretend to go into hiding.

[8] James Reston, in the *New York Times*, July 29, 1958.

9

Public Relations of the Public Trust

> Every channel of communication must contain a flow of information, whether fact or fancy, whether oral, written, or visual. Those who guide and control this flow must either reach out for information and shape it to their needs or accept communications already satisfactorily shaped. Here is where the skill of the professional public relations men comes in.
>
> THOMAS D. YUTZY AND SIMON WILLIAMS*

IN 1952, a small group attached itself to the "Citizens for Eisenhower" movement under the nondescript title of "Eisenhower-Nixon Research Service." Among its members were a former government intelligence agent and an expert on psychological warfare. Their work was devoted to systematically analyzing the news coverage being given the presidential and vice-presidential nominees. They were not so much interested in content as in volume. More particularly, they measured the headline inches and compiled elaborate graphs based on formulas they had worked out. They sent daily bulletins to the Republican campaign trains about the status of the publicity battle, along with suggestions about how to achieve greater front page coverage.

They took no public opinion samplings. But their prediction of the outcome of the election, based exclusively on this study of the mass media, missed the actual voting results by only 1 per cent, a smaller margin of error than was made by any of the leading pollsters.

* In the *Harvard Business Review,* May–June 1955.

Afterward, the Eisenhower-Nixon Research Service set itself up as a permanent organization under the name of "Research Associates" and made a strong effort to sell its services to the new Administration. An elaborate brochure prepared for limited distribution among top government officials declared that "Scientific analysis of public opinion does more than tell the expert what is going on and what to do about it. Effective analysis reveals how to influence the public mind, how to take a perfectly good idea that has somehow failed to go over and make it work."

According to the theory of Research Associates, publicity not only affects public opinion but may simultaneously be used as a yardstick for measuring public opinion. This was the explanation for such preoccupation with the output of the mass media. The brochure contained a number of suggestions about techniques for manipulating publicity. The Administration, it was suggested, should always "pick a spokesman equal to the target." It should time the release of news so as to get the greatest "play," taking special advantage of the general dearth of news on Mondays. It should employ public opinion experts full time in "scanning Democratic news and using every item for a Republican statement." It should use the "judo" principle, which was defined as a "readiness to turn the opponent's lunge into a sprawl."

Research Associates encountered jealousy among the more old-fashioned politicians of the Republican National Committee and failed to gain a place for itself. But traces of this newfangled science it wished to merchandise have appeared repeatedly and provoked serious misgivings. There is plausibility to the proposition that the publicity about government can be subjected to shrewd and possibly unprincipled manipulation.

When James Reston appeared before the Moss Committee investigating the "Availability of Information from Federal

Departments and Agencies," he voiced the uneasiness felt by many:[1]

> Most of my colleagues here have been talking primarily about the suppression of news. I would like to direct the committee, if I may, to an equally important aspect of this problem which I think is the growing tendency to manage the news. Let me see if I can illustrate what I mean:
>
> I think there was a conscious effort to give the news at the Geneva Conference [of the heads of state in 1955] an optimistic flavor. I think there was a conscious effort there, decided upon even perhaps ahead of time for spokesmen to emphasize all the optimistic facts coming out of that conference and to minimize all of the quarrels at that conference with the results which we all have seen.
>
> There was, after the Geneva Conference a decision taken in the Government that perhaps this was having a bad effect, that the people in the Western countries were letting down their guard, and therefore a decision was made, primarily upon the appeal of Chancellor Adenauer of Germany, that the Government should strike another note. So that after the Geneva smiling, the new word went out that it might be a good idea now to frown a little bit, so the President made a speech at Philadelphia, taking quite a different light about the Geneva Conference. That is what I mean by managing the news. And I would urge your committee to look into that a bit, because, while it is bad to suppress a bit of information, it would seem to me to be even worse if all of the newsmaking powers of the Federal Government were to blanket the newspaper situation with the theme which perhaps they did not believe was quite true, but might be an instrument of their thought.

The business of "managing the news" has cropped up in other areas. In 1953, for example, there were a number of telltale signs to indicate that Attorney General Herbert

[1] Hearings before a Subcommittee of the Committee on Government Operations, House of Representatives, 84th Congress, 1st Session, November 7, 1955.

Brownell's attack on former President Truman for "knowingly" promoting a Communist spy, i.e., Harry Dexter White, was part of a carefully planned operation calculated to garner maximum publicity. A short time before Brownell made the attack, the Republican National Committee had ordered fifty thousand reprints of a Senate Internal Security Committee report on "Interlocking Subversion" in which White's name was prominently mentioned.

The timing of the attack was a superb example of the "judo" principle in operation. Brownell made it in a speech before the Chicago Executives Club at approximately 12:30 P.M. Chicago time (1:30 in Washington). Advance texts of two other speeches he gave that day had been distributed to the press the preceding afternoon, but this one, ironically entitled "Ethics in Government," was held up until shortly before Brownell spoke. As a result there was no chance for reporters to alert Truman before the story moved on the press wires and out over radio and television. When frantic calls began to reach him in Missouri, Mr. Truman had to answer fast if he wanted to get his statement into the afternoon papers along with Brownell's charges.

Truman's hurried lunge was quickly turned into a sprawl. He said that he did not remember any FBI memorandum on White and that he had got rid of him when he found that White was "wrong." By four o'clock that afternoon (Washington time), White House Press Secretary James C. Hagerty had called in reporters and made public the text of a Truman letter in 1947 accepting Harry Dexter White's "resignation" and praising him for his services. Hagerty did not bother to explain how a six-year-old letter had been dug out of the files so quickly, still in plenty of time for the evening papers and newscasts.

The G.O.P. publicity director gave this reporter an account of what went on at the Republican National Committee that same afternoon: "We put four men on the telephone to alert members of Congress. Three placed simultaneous calls to Velde, Jenner and McCarthy." Those three gentlemen, of course, were chairmen of the investigating committees which could be counted on to pick up the publicity ball and carry it for an indefinite period.

In the events that followed, there was evidence of managed as well as unmanaged "news developments." That same afternoon, Chairman William Jenner of the Senate Internal Security Committee dispatched subpoenas to key Truman aides. When Chairman Harold H. Velde of the House Un-American Activities Committee tried to get into the act by subpoenaing Truman himself, the Republican publicity director hurriedly talked him out of it. It was felt that pushing the former President too far might provoke public reaction.

Despite the careful publicity planning, the Harry Dexter White affair took a strange turnabout when Senator McCarthy demanded and got free time on a nation-wide radio and television hookup to answer a televised reply Truman had made to Brownell. Instead of answering Truman, however, McCarthy launched a biting attack on the Eisenhower Administration for not being sufficiently tough on Communists.

The whole episode with its farcical climax was a distasteful case study in the misuse of publicity. In all the commotion which occupied the nation's attention for weeks the question was never forcefully raised or answered: Why should a former President of the United States be tried for treason in the headlines?

More and more in recent years the Washington correspondent has been aware of the "managed" news event which he is expected to report without paying attention to the props and staging devices. Too often, he tamely complies with the purpose of the publicists. For a prolonged period Administration spokesmen were able to carry on the fantastic game of juggling the numbers of "security risk" dismissals in such a way as to create a public impression that a wholesale cleanup of subversives in the government was taking place. Diligent reporters compiled documentary proof that the mounting totals furnished to them included a loose compilation of resignations and dismissals on other grounds than security. But it was a complicated story and most reporters were content to play it just the way the government spokesmen wished.

Manipulated news can also be used as an instrument against an Administration. In 1954, leading Democrats raised implications that Eisenhower's friend Bobby Jones had conspired with the President on the golf course to destroy the Tennessee Valley Authority. Jones was supposedly an agent of a private power combine, Dixon-Yates, seeking to invade TVA. The particular charge was utterly without foundation. Yet because it was so sensational it succeeded in returning the Dixon-Yates story to the front pages and, as a direct consequence, revived interest in a lagging congressional investigation. Once again an unsubstantiated attack served to trigger the publicity mechanisms and yield calculated results. The press was used as a vehicle for the transmission of managed news. A complex and important issue was reduced to an absurdity.

⁂

A more subtle case study in government public relations is provided by the recent career of James Hagerty, who, in the opinion of an admiring critic, has been "by every standard the best — and most powerful — White House press secretary in U. S. history . . . Day in, day out, year in, year out, between Presidential speeches and press conferences, during

Eisenhower vacations and Eisenhower illnesses, Hagerty is the authentic voice of the White House and, to an extent rarely recognized, of the whole Administration." [2] The former Assistant to the President, Sherman Adams, has remarked, "Jim has been largely responsible for the complexion of the Administration." According to a newsman, "Jim Hagerty holds a lens ground to his own prescription over the White House — and outsiders have little choice but to look through it."

With Washington reporters, and especially the group who are assigned on a continuous basis to the White House, Hagerty has proved thoroughly skilled and obliging in meeting the vexing demands of their business. He is a superb technician. He knows the strengths and weaknesses of the White House regulars. He knows particularly well their nagging need to produce a steady flow of news. Twice a day and sometimes more he holds informal press conferences in a diligent effort to meet this need.

Hagerty has shown shrewd and farsighted judgment on occasion. When the President was stricken with his heart attack in 1955, passing along the word "Tell Jim to take over," the Press Secretary instituted a publicity operation remarkably candid in view of the grave situation. From dawn till late each evening press conferences were held and medical bulletins issued furnishing fresh news for one edition after another. Heart specialist Paul Dudley White was produced regularly to provide for the reporters intimate medical details about the ailing President. When some Administration officials quailed at a mimeographed handout on the presidential bowels, Hagerty was unconcerned. He flooded the nation with news of the illness and probably helped avert a great deal of public hysteria.

On the other hand, Hagerty is capable of rather subtle judgments in this business of public relations. Less than a

[2] *Time,* January 27, 1958.

year later, when Eisenhower was again hospitalized for the ileitis operation, the Press Secretary was not nearly so obliging to the press. "A presidential heart attack is the property of the people," he explained afterward. "But we did not consider the ileitis something that endangered the President's life."

Hagerty's word has weighed heavily in the inner policy councils. His judgments, like those of most public relations aides, are more on form than on substance. Those who have watched him in action — both in Washington and at various conferences abroad — soon discover that his constant preoccupation is how it will look in print.

All these qualities may be considered virtues in the public relations business. But the underlying suspicion that has disturbed a number of correspondents in Washington has been that Hagerty has carried these virtues too far. He has made of public relations an end in itself rather than a means to an end.

This was most apparent during the prolonged periods when the President has been ill or on vacations. As *Time* Magazine has since reported: [3]

> Hagerty struggled valiantly and, to a point, successfully, in stressing work over play. He took with him on trips briefcases full of executive orders, appointments, etc., and parceled them out daily to make news under the Augusta or Gettysburg dateline. He encouraged feature stories on the Army Signal Corps' elaborate setup to keep Ike in close touch with Washington. He produced Cabinet members in wholesale lots (Does Hagerty really call for Cabinet members? Says he: "Maybe sometimes I do"). He did anything and everything, in short, to keep the subjects of golf and fishing far down in the daily stories about the President.

Hagerty has not been above hocus-pocus. Once, during

[3] *Time,* January 27, 1958.

Eisenhower's illness, he handed a visiting Cabinet member a statement to read to reporters about how well the President was looking. The man had not yet been in to see the President.

Time attempts to rationalize these efforts. "Press Secretary Hagerty cannot by the nature of his job manufacture a presidential record. He can only reflect what President Eisenhower does in its best light." But the trouble is that Hagerty has so arranged the lights and shadows that he has distorted the public image of the President and, more importantly, of the Presidency itself. For prolonged periods, he has attracted public attention away from compelling problems of leadership with a succession of makeshift and inconsequential diversions. His skill has been so great that the editors of at least one major United States newspaper felt obliged to cut down the number of front page stories coming out of the White House because they judged it was causing a false public impression of the President's activities.

With the help of copy-hungry newsmen, Hagerty succeeded for a considerable period in creating the image of a sort of electronic Presidency, super-organized and super-efficient. Great amounts of literature described the *new* National Security Council, the Cabinet secretariat, and the other organizational devices that were supposed to relieve the burdens of the ailing Eisenhower. Yet, as Frederick W. Collins of the Providence *Journal* noted during this period, "Except in rare instances, no outsider knows who in the White House or in the government at large is responsible for a given decision, however diligent his inquiry . . ." The reporter had the feeling that he was being briefed more and more about less and less.

⁊ ⁊ ⁊

There is an ancient and healthy distrust in America of the publicity agent. Congress periodically administers budget slashes aimed at these functionaries in the Executive Branch, though it seems unconcerned about the increasing numbers on its own payroll. At their annual meetings, members of the American Society of Newspaper Editors sound the alarm over the growth of government press agentry. So far, it must be added, they have tended to direct their energies at such obvious and comparatively harmless symptoms as the mimeographed handout, while neglecting more subtle manifestations.

The steady advance of technology stimulates fears from time to time of an era of controlled propaganda. Electronic miracles in communication are now possible in television and radio. Already, for example, the national party headquarters can add ghosted appearances to ghost writing as a technique of campaigning. An aspiring candidate is shown on the television screen engaged in earnest conversation with a prominent Cabinet member. No one need know that he has been dubbed into a prepared film without having met the Cabinet officer in the flesh. When questioned about the ethics of this practice, one of its innovators retorted rather sharply to this reporter: "You don't think anything about it when a Hollywood movie shows the star singing from the back of a horse. Yet you know he actually didn't sing on horseback. What's the difference?" That there might be a distinction to be drawn between Hollywood horse opera and responsible political practice had apparently never occurred to him.

Perhaps the most portentous signs of an Orwellian future may be seen in the great public relations struggle among the armed services. It is a serious business, for at stake are the vast appropriations to be dislodged from Congress with the aid of sympathetic public opinion. In the opinion of the partisans of the Army, the Navy, and the Air Force, public relations is the first line of a fight for survival. In the balance hangs the allocation of the new weapons and the assignment of roles and missions. Words, they proclaim, are weapons, every bit as necessary to survival as guns and planes. "Facts must be convincing, demonstrated, living salesmen of practical benefits," the Air Force has urged its information officers. "These are the only kind of facts that mold opinion and channel the vibrant tensions of public thinking; always deciding issues in the end, altering military policy as surely as defeat in war — they make public opinion the most powerful tool of all, more powerful even than war itself."

Within each armed force, officers holding the rank of major general are in charge of the "Information Services." No technique of appeal through the mass media is neglected. Inspection tours, expenses paid, carry the willing reporter to the far corners of the globe. Magazine articles and books are subsidized. More than one bestseller has brought fame and fortune to a Washington correspondent as a result of "research material" supplied by a service or, in the case of reserve officers, writing performed while returned to a temporary tour of "active duty."

Films, animated cartoons, even the comic strips are the subject of intense armed force competition. The Air Force heaps high honors on Milton Caniff, whose "Terry and the Pirates" and, subsequently, "Steve Canyon" contain unabashed propaganda for this service. The Navy likewise pays tribute to "Buzz Sawyer," while the Army sends intermediaries to plead for kinder treatment from the creators of "Beetle Bailey" and "Sergeant Bilko." An Army P.I.O. has sadly pointed out his service's weakness in determining the kind of war movies shown to the viewing public: "Hollywood regularly produces Technicolor films that are great propaganda for the Air Force and the Navy, but we just don't get the same treatment. After all, they can do without Army cooperation simply by going out and buying a few rifles. But they can't afford to buy their own B-52's or their own aircraft carriers." [4]

The resources of the public relations battle are by no means limited to the Pentagon. For each service there is an "association" bringing together its various patrons and unbound by the strictures against propaganda and lobbying that limit the services themselves. The associations are further back-stopped by the substantial segment of American industry now dependent on defense spending. The "advertisement" paid for by the private industrial firm has become a regular feature of service competition in the rocket and guided missile field.

For the Washington reporter covering the Pentagon, a number of problems are raised by this public relations colossus. More than other places, he finds it difficult to maintain a sense of his own integrity. The subject is so complex. The assistance proffered to him by the armed services can be useful yet insidious. There is a sense of the futility of independent research in the midst of so vast a public relations effort. Among the less able or less purposeful correspondents, many succumb to the spoon feeding. Often they turn into ill-concealed publicists for one armed service or another.

⸎ ⸎ ⸎

From time to time a spokesman from the press issues an undiscriminating blast against the government public relations monster, which he depicts as thwarting the true mission of the press. But it is a mistake, I believe, to think that modern democratic government can ever be neglectful of the processes of publicity. Its importance to the conduct of

[4] William S. Fairfield, "PR for the Services — In Uniform and in Mufti," in *The Reporter*, May 15, 1958.

government is too great. There is realization both here and abroad that publicity must receive some coordination and some direction. In London, British leaders have recently delegated to an ancient sinecure, the Chancellor of the Duchy of Lancaster, the job of handling this task for the Cabinet. In Bonn, the Bundespresse Amt, working directly under the Chancellor, approaches somewhat the same task with German methodicalness. In Washington, where publicity plays a much more immediate and compelling role in government, an Administration is bound to take it into account.

This should not mean the piling up of still vaster government information activities, nor the exploitation of new publicity gimmicks. There is no need for more of the Hagerty-type operation, which, despite its technical proficiency, cannot substitute for the responsible source of explanation at the highest level of government. In his management of news, Hagerty has in fact often discouraged such explanation. He has rebuffed the reporter's efforts to approach other White House sources for briefings on important policy questions. The office of the President has become a no-man's land for the reporter who is seeking guidance on important policy in flux.

What is needed at the highest level of government, as former Senator William Benton once proposed, is a "people's advocate" whose job it is to defend the public's right to know. "He would strive to create a constant presumption in favor of disclosure. He would fight as hard to release information as some officials have been known to suppress it." [5] Of course, he would be concerned with management of the news. His job would be to make certain that the news about government is complete and in focus, not fragmentary and distorted. He would recognize, in the words of Justice Felix Frank-

[5] William Benton, article in *Editor & Publisher,* October 3, 1953.

furter, that "the Presidency is the most important educational system in the country." And, as Frankfurter also said, "democratic government may indeed be defined as the government which accepts in the fullest sense responsibility to explain itself."

10

The Matter of the Truth

> A modern dictator with the resources of science at his disposal can easily lead the public on from day to day, destroying all persistency of thought and aim, so that memory is blurred by the multiplicity of daily news and judgement baffled by its perversion.
>
> WINSTON CHURCHILL*

WHEN ON RARE OCCASIONS, he takes time to review his many mandates, the Washington correspondent is apt to be overwhelmed. His preparation of the news cannot help but be conditioned by the audiences for whom he is writing. Amid competitive and ofttimes contradictory pressures he must somehow achieve a skillful equilibrium. And he must do it, quite frequently, in a white heat of creativity, while the waiting presses set the one unyielding pressure.

There is the audience composed of his sources, the various denizens of the Washington arena, who read his copy with great care and sensitivity. The correspondent who intends to endure must be ever mindful of them. Even the most powerful reporter learns to ration his enemies. For the ordinary reporter, there is often a painful awareness that too open an approach to the news can mean too many closed doors around town.

There is the audience of his bosses. The cupidity of their

* From *The Second World War* (Boston, 1948–53).

influence has been berated and, at times, overrated. It varies, of course, from boss to boss.[1] But the more continuous and compelling pressure upon the Washington correspondent comes from basic economic trends in the communications business. News is big business. News is a commodity that must be purveyed to an ever expanding audience by increasingly monopolistic distributors. It must be homogenized for *Homo* genus in the mass. The reporter in Washington today is continually aware of the economic facts of life that decree how much time and energy he may devote to what pursuits.

There is the audience of his readers, a frenetic group who, he is told, spend eighteen and one-half minutes a day reading five columns of news, of which only one-eighth is international.[2] The reader, it has been said, is the median man, destined, like Orphan Annie, never to grow an inch. His intelligence is such that he must have it explained day after day who is the Secretary of State, but, paradoxically, can be trusted to have highly complex issues described for him in a few terse sentences. It is the median man's attention, not his intelligence, that must be attracted and held. To accomplish this the reporter feels a gnawing compulsion to devise ever more resourceful ways of perfecting the "leads" and "angles" of his stories.

When he is in a philosophical frame of mind, the Washington correspondent asks himself whether news was ever meant to serve as the vehicle for communicating the "truth" about government. Many years ago Walter Lippmann, while still a comparative newcomer to journalism, examined the proposition and reached a pessimistic conclusion. "If we assume . . . that news and truth are two words for the same

[1] I have deliberately avoided getting into the predominantly one-party nature of newspaper ownership. It is a fact of life. Quite frankly, I have no new ideas or information to add on the subject.

[2] Study sponsored by the International Press Institute.

thing, we shall, I believe, arrive nowhere," he wrote.[3] The function of news, Lippmann pointed out, is "to signalize an event," whereas the function of truth is "to bring to light the hidden facts, to set them into relation with each other, and make a picture of reality on which men can act." Lippmann ridiculed the notion that the press, by acting upon everybody for a few minutes each twenty-four hours, "can create a mystical force called Public Opinion that will take up the slack in public institutions."

Yet, this is precisely the job that the Washington correspondent has been called upon to attempt. As the business of government has become more complicated, the responsible reporters have felt a gnawing urge to expose "the hidden facts," to relate them, and to furnish a realistic picture of what is happening. So far, no other institutions of American society have shown a capacity to do the job as well on a day-in-and-day-out basis.

Of course, there have been notable advances in the direction of the "organized intelligence" which Lippmann advocated back in 1922. Within the government, reliable offices such as the Bureau of Labor Statistics provide the framework of statistical facts on which the reporter can base his analyses. The *Congressional Quarterly,* to cite a remarkable privately owned institution, furnishes him useful yardsticks to measure the performance of the various members of Congress. Before it began publication of its voting charts, the reporter had little opportunity to make a systematic comparison between the words and the deeds of the individual Congressman. *CQ* has dealt a valuable blow to hypocrisy.

There have been other significant contributions to "organized intelligence" in the work of the various commissions, advisory groups, study missions, and research organizations in and out of government. They have helped to make the

[3] Walter Lippmann, *Public Opinion* (New York, 1922).

reporter's facts more reliable and to relieve him of that impossible function which Lippmann described as being "the umpire in the unscored baseball game." Today, more than in the past, he has been provided scoring cards and a set of rules for judging the strikes and errors.

Even so, however, there are dilemmas for the reporter. Should he accept the claims of government officials like Robert Cutler that the National Security Council be exclusively trusted with the "organized intelligence" for the nation's high strategy? Are the NSC's secret deliberations and tightly guarded decisions a satisfactory substitute for the public discussion of issues as serious as the Formosa Strait crisis? Certainly neither Lippmann nor most other responsible journalists would deny the reporter's mission to probe and relate the essential facts even in this sensitive area.

Many times the agencies of organized intelligence operate to conceal or distort the issues for the reporter. The Atomic Energy Commission, for example, has released handouts about its "Operation Sunshine," designed to create bright illusions about a deadly dark business. Life and death facts about radioactive fallout have been casually and belatedly made public by means of a commissioner's speech which was too technical to capture public notice until someone like Dr. Ralph Lapp, a scientist-turned-reporter, made the necessary translation. The AEC has at times pretended to tell everything while explaining nothing. Since no satisfactory safeguards exist to make sure the government will freely communicate its organized intelligence even to appropriate officials within government itself, the reporter still has the job of investigating and describing the closest approximation to the truth that he can discover.

The Washington correspondent knows that he has done his job well at times. On occasion, he has stimulated public controversy on misguided policies when even the members of the opposition party had previously maintained a discreet silence. He has broken up petty conspiracies among politicians too long vested with arbitrary power. He has exposed the corruption that both power and the neglectful use of power breeds among politicians. On the positive side, he has served as middleman and broker for important new ideas and policies. He, as much as anyone, has helped to keep Washington in healthy ferment.

The little band of reporters composing the top echelon of the Washington press corps contains men of genuine ability. A number among the seniors — Marquis W. Childs and Raymond P. Brandt of the St. Louis *Post-Dispatch,* Edwin A. Lahey of the Knight Bureau, Richard L. Strout of the *Christian Science Monitor,* James Reston, Arthur Krock, and William H. Lawrence of the *New York Times,* Frederick W. Collins of the Providence *Journal,* Robert J. Donovan and Roscoe Drummond of the New York *Herald Tribune,* Edward T. Folliard and Robert C. Albright of the Washington *Post and Times-Herald,* Gerald E. Griffin and Paul Ward of the Baltimore *Sun,* Carleton Kent and Frederick Kuh of the Chicago *Sun-Times,* Arthur Sylvester of the Newark *News,* Jack Bell and John M. Hightower of the Associated Press, Eric Sevareid, Edward P. Morgan, and Martin Agronsky of the networks, and others — have given status to the business of being a reporter.

Reporters excel in special ways. Chalmers Roberts, of the Washington *Post and Times-Herald,* has no peer in the painstaking detective work of fitting together the bits and pieces of a foreign policy *démarche* to come up with a clear picture of what has happened. Brigadier General (ret.) Thomas R. Phillips, of the St. Louis *Post-Dispatch,* performs much the same function in military affairs. Clark Mollenhoff, of the Cowles papers, has brought new zest to the reporter's ancient tradition of exposing corruption. Charles Bartlett of the

Chattanooga *Times,* while still a young man, won a Pulitzer Prize and eliminated an erring Secretary of the Air Force by a painstakingly researched exposé. William S. White, reporter-turned-columnist, and Rowland Evans, Jr., of the New York *Herald Tribune,* have made congressional politics alive and interesting as a continuing story. Mary McGrory, of the Washington *Evening Star,* adds rare wit to her political reporting.

Reporters have worked to improve the quality of their product. Under the leadership of James Reston, the traditionally stodgy *New York Times* bureau has achieved new standards of capable and readable reporting. Reston has assembled a staff of younger men still unwedded to the pyramid style of newswriting in which all the essentials of the story are crammed willy-nilly into the opening paragraphs. He encouraged his reporter on judicial matters, Anthony Lewis, to spend a year at Harvard Law School, so that now the Supreme Court is no longer a lonely outpost, isolated from competent journalistic coverage. *Times* policy puts an economic analysis by Edwin L. Dale, Jr., on page one because it is the important if not the sensational "news" of the day. *Times* reporters like Russell Baker and E. W. Kenworthy operate with the happy certainty that they have the latitude and, equally important, the space to tell a story the way it deserves.

The *Times* bureau occupies a position of almost frightening ascendancy in the reporting of Washington. But there is competition. Within a dozen smaller bureaus, the keen sense of rivalry with the *Times* adds vigor to the business.

This is by no means a total listing of the highly competent. These reporters and others constitute a select company within the larger ranks of the Washington press corps. They are not incorporated into any special group. Several are still quite junior in the hierarchy. By breeding and background they are highly varied. A number are escapees from family traditions that would ordinarily have led them into the more respectable professions of banking or law. Others come from more modest beginnings. But the good ones are linked by a sense of the importance of what they are doing that compensates for all the limitations in pay, working hours, and high tensions of the business. "Above all, reporting offers the sense of being *engagé* in the political process of one's own time," the Alsop brothers have written. "The reporter who is not consciously *engagé* is in fact likely to be a very bad and unsuccessful reporter." [4]

✓ ✓ ✓

Yet, to anyone who considers the matter, it is a shock to realize just how precarious is the base from which these reporters operate. The constituency to which they communicate about the state of the nation is pitifully small compared to, say, the constituency of the television comedian or the comic-strip artist. Outside Washington, they are not big guys. Most are aware that they are allowed to operate not because of economic benefits they bring in but because their bosses believe it is in the public interest. They are aware, too, that the concepts of what is in the public interest can change. Publications can go to pot almost overnight. Networks can undergo fierce shake-ups.

This role reporters play in Washington must be in large part self-directed. Yet, they lack even a set of guiding principles commonly imposed within the press corps to satisfy the ethical exigencies. "Shyster lawyers can be disbarred, quack doctors can have their licenses revoked, and unworthy ministers can be unfrocked, but the newspaper profession had no method of dealing with black sheep," wrote a disgruntled critic about an earlier period in Washington. The

[4] Joseph and Stewart Alsop, *The Reporter's Trade* (New York, 1958).

profession has few methods even today. The Nieman Foundation at Harvard and other endowed cultivators of excellence have raised standards to which the high-minded may rally. But reporters still have reason to believe that too high principles may frustrate chances of success. Too often the monetary rewards go to those who find in journalism a different kind of challenge.

Finally, the reporter in Washington has had to consider the subject matter with which he deals daily. He has watched politics — the stuff of his trade — explode like the now familiar mushroom cloud, engulfing economics, military strategy, and at last the worlds of nuclear and space science. He suspects darkly that somewhere along the way the essentials of a reporter's knowledge moved into a new order of magnitude. He harks back nostalgically to the time when the subjects government dealt with did not seem so alien or formidable to the gifted amateur. Now all that has changed. He feels he ought to know almost everything to report with a fair degree of accuracy about anything. Even so technical a subject as Strontium 90 can become of a sudden a political fact to be hurled at him. The reporter finds himself caught in an insufferable bind between the scientist and the politician and his readers.

Is he up to the enormous challenge that confronts him? As the reporters in Washington survey the product of all their labor, the honest ones sometimes feel despairingly that more and more is being written about less and less. Despite the size of the press corps, the vast paraphernalia at its disposal, and all the government facilities for dispensing information, there is growing awareness of the perilous state of our communications. Yet, hopefully, there is also a new sense of awareness that our very survival as a free nation may depend on the capacity of reporters to relate the essential truth, and "make a picture of reality on which men can act."

Postscript

The Moscow Dateline — An Experiment in Controlled Fission of News

WE LEARN much about ourselves by the study of opposites. Both in theory and in practice the Soviet press is the antithesis of ours. The opportunity to observe the reporters at work in Moscow had for me the beneficial effect of bringing into sharper focus the role played by the reporters in Washington. Though not intended as part of the thesis of the book, I have attempted here to set down as a postcript this account of the tightly regulated publicity process that lies behind the Moscow dateline.

The first horrifying fact to confront the visiting reporter in Moscow is that he cannot lay his hands on that essential tool of his trade, the telephone directory. To locate a telephone number he must make a trip to the central post office, where an ancient and incomplete directory is kept. What is more, government departments do not have central switchboards. Unless the reporter happens to know the particular number of the official with whom he wishes to communicate, he is helpless.

Top information officer in Moscow, when I visited there in 1958, was a Mr. Ilyichev, in the External Affairs Ministry. Yet not a single American correspondent of the dozen I interviewed in Moscow knew his telephone number or had ever been able to reach him directly. Their principal contact in the Ministry was a Mr. Bezmerny, a youthful assistant far down the hierarchy, who upon being reached after great difficulty habitually refused to answer the most insignificant inquiry until he checked with his superiors. He might or might not call back. While I was in Moscow, Western correspondents waited in vain for confirmation or denial of the widespread rumor that Georgi Malenkov had been killed in a power-station accident.

Here is only the beginning of the foreign reporter's problems in Moscow. His means of access to the news is blocked to the point of total frustration. There is no system of background briefings. The reporter pursues confidential informants at his own risk except among the Embassy officials whose information may be scarcely more reliable than his own. On rare occasion he is summoned to a "press conference" at which an official announces what the government wishes to make public but allows no real cross-examination by the press.

For the most part, the correspondent's job is a deadly dull routine. He spends his morning perusing the Soviet publications with the aid of a translator. He searches for the stray nugget of important information which may be buried deep in an official speech. He scans the gatherings of the Soviet leaders to detect, if only by omission, any shifts in the pecking order of the hierarchy. Sometimes the most significant happenings have been forecast by this painstaking scrutiny of the Communist rituals. The late evenings he must spend in the Central Telegraph Office, where there are the endless delays and numerous deletions imposed by the censor. He knows that even the limited enterprise permitted him is subject to this final control. He tries to forget the kind of enterprise he learned to associate with journalism elsewhere. In Moscow, it could only lead to the revocation of his right to live and work in the Soviet capital.

✓ ✓ ✓

The Soviets declare firmly that they believe in freedom of the press. They cite their constitution which provides, "The citizens of the USSR are granted by law . . . freedom of the press [and] these civil rights are insured by placing at the disposal of the working people and their organizations printing presses, stocks of paper . . . and other material requisites." They point pridefully to the burgeoning of mass communications under Soviet rule. Newspaper circulation, for example, increased thirteen-fold between 1913 and 1956, and amounts today to more than 54 million copies, dailies, weeklies, and random publications combined. *Pravda* alone has a circulation of 5½ million. Tass, the Soviet wire service, receives a daily incoming file of more than 1½ million words — greater in volume than that of the Associated Press.

But the American reporter and the Soviet reporter are operating under two quite fundamentally different concepts of the role of the press. Soviet leaders have made no bones about this. Lenin once declared: "A newspaper is not only a collective propagandist and collective agitator; it is also a collective organizer." And Stalin: "The press should grow not by the day but by the hour, for it is the sharpest and most powerful weapon of our Party." And Khrushchev: "The press is our chief ideological weapon. It is called upon to rout the enemies of the working class, the enemies of the toilers. Just as an army cannot fight without weapons, so the Party cannot successfully carry on its ideological work without such a sharp and militant weapon as the press."

In ideology and in practice, no separation between press and state exists in the Soviet system. As Mr. N. G. Palgunov, managing director of Tass, has explained, "There cannot be an opposition press because there are no antagonistic classes in the Soviet Union. Everybody has the same ideas and struggles for the same standard of social life."

This concept of the role of the press inevitably produces a definition of news which sounds absurd to the Westerner. "In the Soviet Union . . . not events but social processes are treated as news and regarded as being newsworthy," one analyst has written. "The major, and in a sense virtually the only, news item in the Soviet Union is the process called socialist construction, that is, the general effort to build up Soviet society."[1] The managing director of Tass defined "news" in a journalism lecture given at the University of Moscow: "Unlike the bourgeois press, we are interested only in facts. The Tass reporter must follow the struggle of the classes; but he must do it objectively." Then he added, "It is not enough to give a fact if it is not connected with something useful. It is no use giving the theory of Pythagoras unless it has a meaning to it."

News is a highly impersonal thing. Individuals, except as they play a symbolic part in "socialist construction," have literally no news interest. Former Senator William Benton pointed out, after a study tour in the Soviet Union, the interesting case of the coal miner Stakhanov, who during the 1930's performed extraordinary production feats with his drill. Stakhanovism became a familiar household word in the U.S.S.R. Yet despite the tremendous publicity play, no news accounts ever provided interesting details about the man himself. While I was in Moscow, I requested permission to gather facts for a story about Premier Khrushchev's family life. Mr. Yuri Zhukov, head of the Cultural Exchange Com-

[1] Alex Inkeles, *Public Opinion in Soviet Russia* (Cambridge, 1951).

mittee, told me disdainfully that the Soviet people were not interested in prying into the personal affairs of their leaders.

There is a timeless quality about Soviet news. The event can be reported weeks or months or even years after it has happened. As Tass Director Palgunov has argued rather belligerently, "Fact is a Latin word and it means that which actually happened . . . Tass makes no attempt to pass out for facts what are merely reasonable suppositions . . . Tass reports facts only when they really are facts . . ."

Facts can be slow in developing. In 1956, the Soviet press hesitated for days before carrying word of the Hungarian revolt. In 1957, the decision of the Communist Party Central Committee against Comrades Molotov, Kaganovich, Malenkov and Shepilov was delayed four days before publication. Toward the latter part of 1957, a Soviet naval officer who sought refuge in West Berlin told of a major ship in the Soviet fleet which had sunk near the Crimea in 1955, causing about 1500 deaths. Not one word of the accident appeared in the Soviet press. Khrushchev's famous speech to the Twentieth Party Congress, in which he denounced Stalin, has been read orally in public meetings all over the country but never published in the newspapers.

This rigidly *ex post facto* approach to the news considerably simplifies the pressures on the Soviet editor. It enables the newspaper to prepare a detailed plan of the content and layout sometimes a month in advance and to have as much as 50 per cent of each current issue set in type and made up several days before the issue date.[2]

The Soviet newspaper provides monotonous reading. Day after day the front page of *Pravda* or *Izvestia* is dominated by long pronouncements by one or another of the Soviet leaders. Half a page may be devoted to Soviet achievements

[2] Inkeles, *Public Opinion.*

in the field of construction industries. A detailed account is given of the production norms for a faraway dam project. As much as 75 to 80 per cent of the newspaper can be taken up with such government handouts. Usually on page four (or page six if it is a six-pager), one finds the foreign news judged suitable for the Soviet reader. The whole paper reads like a company house organ which, in fact, is pretty much what it is.

The situation has changed a bit since Stalin's time. Then *Pravda* would run a twenty-two-month serial of the greetings sent the Premier on his seventieth birthday. By the time it was completed Stalin was approaching seventy-two. In 1953, Nikita Khrushchev issued a blast against the "firmly fixed sterotypes and well worn methods whereby everything is written according to a simple pattern." He demanded that "materials must be more varied, and more thought must be given to content and form of exposition." Students of the Soviet press have noted some improvement in style and format, but, significantly, *Soviet Press,* the professional publication of the Journalists' Union, still interprets Khrushchev's demand to mean "bringing the most important development and events of our life to the broadest mass of readers and helping them to understand and *draw the right* conclusions" (italics mine).

What does the Soviet reader get out of his newspaper? The sales indicate he buys it regularly and visitors can observe that he reads it with apparent attention. His problems are precisely the opposite of the American newspaper reader. The American must contend with encapsulated news, often fragmented to the point of unintelligibility; the Soviet must wade through columns of dreary prose in a vain attempt to find anything truly newsworthy. There is no helpful assist from the Soviet editor to guide the reader. The important part of a story may be buried deep in an official text. The reader must look for the news in strange places. First indication that Police Chief L. P. Beria had met a grim fate at the hands of his comrades came in a "society" announcement. A list of important Soviet leaders attending the opening of an opera failed to include his name. It turned out later that he was already incarcerated.

In this reversed image form of journalism, the intelligent Soviet citizen must learn as much from what is not in his newspaper as from what is there. The minor functionary in Moscow learns, for example, that Marshal Georgi Zhukov has returned from a trip to Yugoslavia. Though his departure had been treated with great fanfare, there is only the barest mention of his return. It does not take too much practice in Soviet readermanship for everyone to suspect Zhukov has fallen out of favor.

Visiting experts in the Soviet Union have noted occasions when an entire issue is quickly sold out because of an apparently inconsequential story tucked away in the paper. In the summer of 1957, a brief news item in *Pravda* mentioning a decree against speculators caused a great flurry at the news stands. Its meaning was lost on the foreigner, but the Soviet reader evidently perceived deeper implications.

The system of control over the Soviet press seems at first glance uncomplicated compared to the massive bureaucracies erected by other totalitarian systems. There is no propaganda ministry in the government. Premier Khrushchev gets along without a press secretary. Formally, censorship is carried out by an agency known euphemistically as Glavlit, or the Literary Bureau. The informal control is much more pervasive. Major propaganda lines are carefully worked out in a department of the Communist Party known as Agitprop. Editors of party papers must be party members and the others, according to the Communist Central Committee, must display "a fundamental Bolshevik firmness and organizational capacity, the ability aggressively and at the required pace to organize the masses in the resolution of the basic tasks of socialist construction." The editor of *Pravda* and the managing director of Tass are both members of the Communist Central Committee and presumably privy to what is happening at the top levels of government.

Soviet editors are reluctant to discuss the degree of central direction over the press. Mr. Palgunov denied to William Benton that Tass sent out instructions to the provincial editors about the handling of news. Benton then picked at random three newspapers from a stack on Palgunov's desk. Each carried exactly the same headline across the lefthand two columns, and the same picture across the bottom of page one. Palgunov attributed this to "coincidental" news judgment on the part of the editors.

The existence of a tight control over news can be traced in the often bizarre handling of important stories. From the beginning the treatment of the A-bomb story revealed a strange sense of news judgment. Initial announcement of the Hiroshima explosion in 1945 was tucked away in a Tass dispatch from Washington at the bottom of page one in all papers, while the big headline of the day announced "Polish Republic Awards Highest Honors to Marshals of the Soviet Union G. K. Zhukov and K. K. Rokossovsky." The Nagasaki bombing three days later went unmentioned.

News reaches the Soviet readers in roundabout fashion. In 1949, Soviet citizens learned that their government had managed to stage an atomic explosion by means of a Tass dispatch which began, "On September 23, President Truman announced that . . ." The first hint that the Soviets were working on an atomic bomb had been contained in the text of a speech by Molotov in 1947 in which he simply remarked that "the secret of the bomb has long ceased to exist." Two years later, when the Russian bomb was actually exploded,

Tass smugly called attention to Molotov's earlier statement.[3]

A great deal of information is learned through Soviet press denials. In early 1959, *Pravda* denounced as a hoax the United States government's release of the transcribed recording on the shooting down of an American plane in the Caucasus. Only in this oblique way did the Soviet reader learn that the United States had been protesting the disappearance of its flyers.

It would be a mistake to consider that the Soviet press is entirely a carbon copy of government policy. Both in the central Moscow and in the provincial papers, the responsibility of the press for *samokritika,* or self-criticism, is widely publicized. The press has developed a broad network of *rabsel'kor,* or peasant and worker correspondents. The *rabsel'kor* is "not called and not elected but voluntarily takes upon himself the social responsibility of informing the press." In his amateur dispatches and in the letters to the editor columns, there is opportunity to point out abuses in the functioning of government. The Communist Party puts great emphasis on this function of the press and frequently criticizes editors who have been neglecting it.

In terms of volume alone, this self-criticism is quite impressive. A deputy editor of *Pravda* told me quite proudly that his newspaper received over 600,000 letters a year. A sizable staff on each Soviet newspaper works at processing this mail, checking complaints with the appropriate government officials, and notifying the complainant of remedial action to be taken.

The area of permissible criticism appears to be tightly delimited. Activities of top Soviet leaders rarely fall within that area, except when one of them has been dislodged from power and the Soviet public is being readied for his condemnation. Then it is simply a case of echoing decisions already

[3] Leo Graliow in *The Reporter,* March 24, 1955.

taken within the party hierarchy. Across the country there is suddenly an amazing groundswell of editorial reaction against the prejudged official.

In 1956 the Communist Party magazine, *Partiinaya Zhizn* (Party Life), attempted somewhat confusingly to define the limits of editorial discretion. "If the editor disagrees with the Party committee, he is permitted, under Party statutes, to raise the question in the committee and, if necessary, in a superior Party body; but he has no right to use the newspaper to settle personal differences with the Party committee." To confuse matters further, the magazine added, "The newspaper certainly has the right to criticize anyone, but in doing so it must not oppose itself to the District Committee." Much harm could be done by "careless criticism."

This limitation on criticism is a sensitive subject to Soviet editors. In one interview after another, I pressed a number of them to spell out the degree of their autonomy. Each insisted that his editorial judgments were arrived at independently. How had there been such remarkable unanimity over the dismissal of Zhukov or the post-mortem condemnation of Stalin? Their replies were evasive. Would not the press have served a useful function to criticize Stalin while he was still alive, when criticism might have done some good? One editor gave the only frank answer. "The trouble with Stalin," he said, "was that he sent off anyone who tried to criticize him." How, in the absence of press criticism, could one be sure that Khrushchev might not develop the same intolerant attitude as Stalin? The answer was uniformly doctrinaire. Stalin had been guilty of creating "the cult of the personality." By identifying this disease, the editors assured me, the Soviets had eliminated it. No amount of argument could shake this position.

To anyone familiar with the many decisions involved in the business of journalism, it is obvious that the Soviet press, no matter how well coordinated, cannot be free from stresses and strains. Since Stalin's death, the power balance at the very top of the Communist hierarchy has shifted perceptibly from time to time. How can the editor be certain that the word he gets is the final one?

Two conditioned reflexes of Soviet life provide a partial answer. First, the contending leaders in time of dispute do not look upon publicity as a weapon to be employed for resolving the dispute. There has been no recorded case when a high Communist, fearing a fall from power, attempted to take his appeal to the public in the manner of countless American politicians. Second, the Soviet editor, unlike his American counterpart, when in doubt prints nothing. Today, even as in the Stalin era, silence is the telltale symptom of policies and personalities in conflict.

This itself can create communication problems of which the American is only dimly aware. In a modern, highly technical society such as the Soviets are attempting to build, conflicts arise regularly for which the silent treatment is no solution.

Quite regularly the Soviet press feels obliged to denounce the "rumor mill" that seems to operate with great facility despite the controls over the flow of news. Last year when the papers failed to announce a general price cut, usually an annual event, the uncontrollable rumors about a ruble devaluation soon led to a buying spree. The absence of legitimate news evidently does not restrain the public imagination. Particularly, it creates enormous difficulties in any communications among the different countries of the Soviet Empire. In Warsaw, where even the Communists still speak, if not write, with a Western-oriented vocabulary, a Polish Communist editor described to me the dilemmas arising for someone in his position. A Chinese Communist newspaper had just launched a violent attack on Tito. Had the Chinese decided to initiate this new ideological drive entirely on their own? Was it part of a major Soviet offensive? Or was it perhaps a devious effort by Chinese Communists to warn the Soviet leaders that Chinese interests were being neglected? The Warsaw editor frankly admitted that he must weigh each of these possibilities in determining how to treat the story. Even though his copy is subjected to prior censorship, he cannot count on guidance from the censor on such subtle policy matters.[4] Yet, any article or editorial appearing in his paper is studied with the same care in other parts of the Soviet empire that he had given the Chinese editorial. The lot of the Polish editor, even though he is a devout Communist, can be a trying one at times, the Warsaw editor confessed.

Since Stalin, there has been at least one innovation bringing a degree of greater flexibility to Soviet communications. Khrushchev's use of the cocktail party press conference has served as a crude counterpart to the American President's press conference and the British Question Period in the House of Commons. It is hardly an interpellative arrangement, for even the placing of questions is entirely at the Premier's discretion. Instead, it more resembles the practice of an ancient feudal court in which the baronial lord proclaims his dicta amid the merrymaking. Foreign correspondents in Moscow are freely admitted to these social gatherings with the Soviet Premier. They may observe, they may indeed take out their notebooks and cameras and record what transpires. On occasion they may even interrogate. At least the elemental requirements of reporting are met.

What is Khrushchev's purpose? It would appear that in a canny way he senses the same necessity that Western leaders feel to discuss policy initiatives without resorting to the

[4] In the satellite capitals, there is formal censorship of the internal press but not of the foreign correspondents.

starkly defined official proclamation. At the social convocation he can hint at changes in progress. He can issue sly rebuttals to Western declarations. He can manifest anger, contempt, and the thousand and one nuances of mood that are used to convey meaning to the diplomats.

Despite his much publicized consumption of vodka at these conferences — a hazard not faced by the President or the Prime Minister — Khrushchev risks little by this informal communication. The censor is still vigilant and discriminating. Quite frequently, the version which reaches the Soviet reader is markedly different from the one allowed to be sent abroad. At a Polish Embassy reception in Moscow which I attended, the Soviet Premier held forth volubly on Soviet relationships with the Jews, a subject which he brought up quite casually and without relation to anything that had gone before or came afterward. It was reported in some detail in the *New York Times,* but not one word about it appeared in *Pravda.*

✓ ✓ ✓

For the American press Moscow coverage presents a dilemma for which there are no easy solutions. How does the reporter do his job without becoming the unwitting instrument of Soviet propaganda? His every instinct for good reporting is subjected to continual frustration. He has little opportunity for initiative; indeed, his stay in Moscow is apt to be abruptly terminated if he attempts to pursue a story too relentlessly.

Even when he chances upon real news, he finds that censorship is unreasoning and unreasonable. The long evenings spent at the Central Telegraph Office teach a dreary discipline. His copy disappears behind closed doors to be dissected by a censor he never sees. It may be detained ten minutes or two days. Alternatively, it may never reappear. Yet the death of a story, as one Moscow correspondent has noted, is not always permanent. A week later the censors may quickly clear the same dispatch without a word to explain their change in policy.[5]

There is never any explanation. Officially the censor works to insure accuracy in the stories about the Soviet Union. The censor's job, I was told by the dean of the Moscow University Department of Journalism, is to prevent lies from being transmitted — a commendable objective in this academician's view. In practice, factually inaccurate reports are frequently allowed to pass if they reflect credit on the Soviet Union. On the other hand, completely accurate dispatches are blocked because they reveal something which is unfavorable. Even direct quotation of an official Soviet source from an earlier period may not be censor-proof. Past policy is supposed to be forgotten policy if the line has shifted.

The censor can be whimsical. When Marshal Zhukov was dismissed as Defense Minister, one correspondent speculated erroneously that he might receive the post of Premier or Vice-Premier. The censor eliminated only the "Premier" from the story, thus arousing speculation among the reporters that he was giving a gratuitous tip. It turned out he was little concerned with accuracy but simply desired to prevent speculation about Premier Bulganin's incumbency.

At times, the censor appears to be deliberately vindictive. The reporter's copy may be detained for hours after the Soviet radio has already broadcast the identical news to the world. Frustrated foreign correspondents in Moscow often accuse the Soviet officialdom of deliberate efforts to make their tenure unendurable.

[5] Daniel Schorr. "Focus of the Kremlin's Secrecy Obsession," in the *New York Times Magazine*, August 17, 1958.

Distortion of the news is inherent in the Soviet system. The American correspondent in Moscow recognizes the constant danger and makes regular efforts to insure that his editor at least is forewarned. But several of the reporters I interviewed also voiced concern that the obligations imposed on them by Western-style journalism increase rather than lessen the perils of Moscow reporting. Competition for headlines only plays into the hands of the Communists.

The zeal for carrying the Moscow dateline goes to strange limits in our press. A story about the Soviet Union may be picked up in Rome or Warsaw or London. The Moscow correspondent is pestered with incessant telephone calls asking for confirmation, even though he lacks the means of confirming or denying it. Frequently a press agency will have the story completely written in London awaiting only the word of its Moscow bureau that it has been "confirmed." Pressure on the bureau mounts to an intolerable peak. In just such a situation, the Associated Press sent out the completely erroneous dispatch that the Russians had launched a man into space in one of their rockets. Anxious to move it ahead of their competitors, the Moscow bureau had confirmed it on the basis of pure gossip.

The special correspondents in Moscow have similar problems. While I was there, one of the two-member *New York Times* bureau was obliged to stay up until early morning awaiting the censor's clearance of an official Khrushchev communique which had been released many hours earlier in Washington. The *Times*'s Washington bureau could have reported the communiqué with far more meaningful interpretation than would be permissible for the Moscow correspondent. Yet even this distinguished newspaper was obsessed with the importance of nailing its stories to their point of origin.

The present usage of the American press corps in Moscow is wasteful of limited talent. Of the twelve or more correspondents who have been accredited by the Soviets on a permanent basis, only half had received more than the most meager language training before their current assignments. Caught in the routine of their work, most American reporters never get beyond a fairly limited version of Russian. They must rely on interpreters for everything but the elementals of daily conversation.

It needs a minimum of two men to handle a difficult story from Moscow, one working at his office and the other at the Central Telegraph Bureau, where the censor is located. All too often the entire press corps, wire services, and special correspondents may be involved in reporting the same trivial story based on a government handout. It would be far better, one reporter told me, if the special correspondents were permitted by their editors to ignore the routine news stories being handled by the wire services and were encouraged instead to travel about the country reporting the off-beat but frequently more significant stories. He was not certain how long the Soviets would permit it, but he felt that there was no harm in trying.

Among the Moscow correspondents I found a certain cynicism about the uses to which they are put. One wire-service reporter remarked that his agency cared more about preserving its Moscow dateline than the accuracy of his dispatches. He had been instructed quite bluntly that his first responsibility is to maintain his accreditation. It is scarcely an incentive for courageous journalism.

* * *

For the Soviets the Moscow dateline provides a Communist version of government by publicity which has managed to inform and direct an increasingly literate population. Soviet mass communications, in fact, represent an experiment in the controlled fission of literacy. Since Stalin, the use of the secret police terror and intimidation has been reduced as the major instrument of control; the instrument of propaganda has assumed a more critical role in coercing Soviet society. How long and how well their monolithic mass media will serve this purpose is impossible to predict.

For the free world the Moscow dateline is baffling. There is disturbing evidence that Soviet leaders have systematically attempted to use it to send out the predetermined signals by which, in accordance with Pavlovian theory, they hope to create a conditioned reflex in their enemies.

Curiously, the press in quite different ways is indispensable to government in both Washington and Moscow. In the steady drumfire of propaganda warfare between free world and Communist it may be argued that the Soviet press offers the more relentless and effective weapon. There is reason for hope, however, that over the long run it will not provide the basis for the more durable society.